PREPARED FOR DISASTER

A PRACTICAL GUIDE TO PREPARING FOR DISASTERS AND EMERGENCIES

STEVE NEILL

WWW.DISASTER.ZONE

Published in the United States of America

Print version: January 2017 (4th revision)

Cover design: Whistlecraft Design, whistlecraft.com

ISBN-13: 978-1530587223

ISBN-10: 1530587220

Mailing address:

PO Box 632162

Littleton, CO 80163

USA

Email:	info@disaster.zone
Website:	www.disaster.zone
Facebook:	www.disaster.zone/facebook
YouTube:	www.disaster.zone/youtube

Dedication

*To all the hard working disaster response volunteers
and humanitarians I know and love.*

*Our shared experiences and your valuable insights
have taught me much as we work hard to bring relief
to disaster victims around the world.*

*You are the unsung heroes of events
we wish would never happen.*

Community volunteers, Democratic Republic of the Congo

Contents

Introduction

"The actual threat is not nearly as important
as the level of preparation."
— Dr. Alexis Artwohl & Loren W. Christensen

Thank you for buying this book. I really do appreciate it!

I care deeply about what disasters do to people and I want to be part of the solution. My hope is that *"Prepared for Disaster"* will create genuine value by passing on to you the insights, knowledge and experience I have gained. At the same time, proceeds from the sale of this book will help me continue my work as a volunteer disaster responder. So again, thank you!

Following a disaster such as a hurricane, wildfire, earthquake, volcanic eruption, flood, or an act of terrorism, could you and your family be self-sufficient for at least three to seven days, or even longer?

Disasters usually happen without warning. In many parts of the world they are a regular fact of life. They can strike a community at any moment, day or night. A normal day can quickly turn ugly and be like no other you've experienced.

Within seconds, your whole world is literally shaken by an earthquake leaving incredible devastation in its wake. Buildings collapse leaving scores of people buried beneath the rubble of their homes and places of work. All of a sudden panic breaks out, leaving people bewildered and confused. *"How is this happening to us... to me?"*

Disasters wreak havoc, damaging homes and businesses, disabling vital infrastructure such as roads, water supplies, power lines and communications. Important facilities such as hospitals and clinics are overwhelmed and unable to function as normal. Supply chains that deliver food, fuel and other essential resources are damaged or cut-off. In such events thousands of people are affected. In an instant, lives are turned upside-down and without a plan of action, left unprepared. Scores of people are forced to fend for themselves, relying on handouts or reduced to scavenging for basic needs.

Although many disasters are unpredictable, their outcomes have been well studied and are known to follow predictable patterns. By learning from the past we are better able to face the future. Being able to provide your own food, water, shelter, basic first aid, and sanitation can make the difference between life and death, not only for yourself, but for the lives of your family, neighbors and others within your community.

I wrote *"Prepared for Disaster"* with the average person in mind — the type of person who wants to be better prepared for a disaster but isn't sure where to begin. I also wanted to present steps that most people can take without breaking the bank. Yes, it really is possible to prepare for a disaster without looking like a fanatic or going broke by stockpiling masses of supplies! The advice I present is for the everyday person like you and me.

I begin by presenting an overview of disasters (sections 1 to 5) followed by a number of basic steps you can take to prepare for them (sections 6 to 21). These steps will help you cultivate a *"preparedness mindset"* by suggesting simple habits which will serve to improve your wellbeing following a disaster. Other steps are about learning skills that may one day be literal life savers, and some are recommendations for the types of equipment and resources you should acquire to improve your chances of survival. The steps are organized into general categories such as water, food, shelter, and communications. In sections 22-23 I list the practical things you can do when confronted with a very real and immediate threat.

No step by itself will be enough to fix every problem you may encounter, but rather a steady accumulation of good practice, knowledge, skill and specific resources will increase your capacity to withstand the effects of a disaster.

My suggestion is that you first study all the steps and then selectively implement a few each week. Do the easy ones first and make plans to do the others that are more involved or require greater financial commitment later. It's better to build gradually than be too ambitious and quickly lose enthusiasm. Within a few months you'll be well on the way to having a great disaster preparedness plan for you and your family, and become an asset to your community.

Finally, at the very end of the book I have provided handy worksheet pages you can photocopy, complete, and keep in your wallet or purse, or give to family members.

Before we dive in, let me first state that *"Prepared for Disaster"* is **not** ...

- **About survival techniques.** I'm not going to teach you how to start a fire by rubbing sticks together or how to build a snow-cave. There are many excellent books available on such topics but I won't go into those kinds of detail.

- **A comprehensive manual on disaster preparedness** — the emphasis being on *"comprehensive"*. Actually, such a book does not exist! Disasters by their very nature are unpredictable and dynamic. No one book could possibly address every conceivable scenario. At best, you can learn enough to be prepared for *most* disasters, but not *every* disaster! Therefore, use this book as a way to get your disaster preparedness plan off the ground and not as an exhaustive list of *everything* that must be done.

- **Written for North Americans only.** The vast majority of disaster preparedness websites and books seem to focus largely on North American disasters, brands, products, organizations, laws, etc. My experience as a humanitarian volunteer has taken me all over the world to countries including Romania, Thailand, Myanmar, Haiti, Costa Rica and Switzerland. Therefore, I wrote this book as an attempt to break free from this North American-focused myopia and serve a global audience. The fact is, in 2015 alone, disasters affected the lives of almost 99 million people worldwide, claiming over 22,000 lives and causing US$66.5 billion of economic damage[1] making this a truly global problem!

- **Enough to guarantee your safety.** If all you do is read this book but take no action you will have gained some head knowledge and that's about all. Start implementing several steps per week and put your personal disaster preparedness plan into action.

The idea of this book is to help guide you through the practical steps needed to become prepared for a disaster. Therefore, as you read through this book feel free to highlight sections that you feel are important. Make notes and jot down ideas you can apply to your specific situation.

---

[1] www.unisdr.org/we/inform/publications/47804

Finally, please visit my website at **www.disaster.zone** where you will discover more disaster preparedness tips and ideas. The site is being continually developed so feel free to keep coming back and make suggestions on how it can be improved. If you want to get in touch you can email me at info@disaster.zone

For your convenience, you can also use your smartphone or tablet computer to scan the QR codes within this book to get more information from our website.

OK, with all that out of the way let's get started…

1. What is a Disaster?

"Here's a rule of life:
You don't get to pick what bad things happen to you."
— Rory Miller

Let's begin with a few definitions so we know exactly what we're talking about.

A ***disaster*** is a non-routine and catastrophic event that poses large-scale risk to human life and property. Furthermore, a disaster is any event that overwhelms existing resources to deal with that event, resulting in widespread destruction and distress.

Disasters occur when vulnerable people are directly exposed to a specific hazard or threat (e.g. an earthquake, flood, storm, wildfire, war, etc.) and are ill equipped to respond to the harmful effects that hazard creates. These hazards may have existed for a long time or represent a new threat.

A disaster event is usually sudden and unexpected, or occurs with little or no warning, or time to prepare. Typically, following such an event, the community is unable to return to normal without outside assistance. The cost of a disaster is usually counted in terms of lives lost, damage to the health of a population, damage to infrastructure and property, or damage to the environment.

By contrast, an **emergency** is a more geographically isolated event that can be handled by local emergency services and does not have wider social consequences. Much of the advice presented in this book can be applied to disasters and emergency situations alike.

Disasters and emergencies are classified by their type and cause. The type of event influences the nature of the response and in some countries may have implications on how the local or national government may reimburse for property loss.

Traditionally, disasters were classified simply as **natural** and **man-made**. However, today's global and regional disasters do not easily fit these categories. When we consider the contributing causes of disasters, such as increased globalization and population size, climate-change, widespread environmental degradation, poverty and inequality, bad management and weak governance, the lines become blurred.

For example, we may try to decide the true cause of a flood. Was the flood due to heavy rains, or was it because of poor farming practices leading to the loss of topsoil and vegetation? Or was it perhaps a failure of flood defenses due to poor engineering or management?

The contemporary terms used to define the types of disasters are:

- Natural
- Technological and accidental
- Epidemics and pandemics
- Intentional violence and acts of terror

Pause for a few moments and imagine how you might react in the following situations. Put yourself in the shoes of someone who must keep themselves and their family safe when faced with these challenging scenarios:

Scenario #1: A Winter Storm

A freak snowstorm has forced the closure of suburban streets and main arterial roads. Scores of motorists are stranded in their vehicles as a blizzard with record snowfalls cut off many small towns and communities. Many businesses have been forced to close. Unable to leave their homes for several days, residents are running out of fresh food. Wintry blasts have left thousands of people without electricity. Extensive property damage has been reported as local authorities open emergency shelters with the cooperation of the Red Cross.

Scenario #2: An Act of Terrorism

In the heat of summer, an act of terrorism has severely disrupted the main water supply. Until the nature and full extent of the damage is established, authorities have ordered residents to shut off water coming into their homes. Panic buying has emptied the shelves of water at the local supermarkets which are unable to keep up with demand. Some retailers have been accused of price gouging. Army and civilian engineers have been mobilized to repair the damage and restore supplies to normal but this may take several weeks. Several wildfires have been reported on the outskirts of the city — it is uncertain how they started but flames, rumors, and fear are spreading.

Scenario #3: An Earthquake

A massive earthquake has struck in the early hours of the morning. Emergency services, quick to respond are soon overwhelmed with the huge number of casualties trapped in their homes. The cell phone service is overloaded and many local landline numbers are unreachable. A number of key bridges and tunnels are severely damaged. Reports of gas leaks and damaged power lines are stretching the capacity of utility companies. The government has issued a state of emergency and appealed to the public for calm.

Scenario #4: A Hurricane

The weather service is warning of a huge hurricane expected to make landfall within 36 hours. People living in low-lying coastal areas have been advised to seek shelter inland. Residents are hastily securing their homes but building suppliers are running out of plywood and other materials. Many people leaving the area are causing some roads to become congested. The authorities are responding to reports of vehicle accidents as other motorists wait in long lines to obtain fuel.

Scenario #5: A Train Derailment

During a school day in the heat of summer, a train on the outskirts of town has derailed. Emergency services are on the scene and have determined the risk of a possible toxic chemical cloud. Residents are warned via local T.V. and radio to *shelter-in-place*. As a precaution, the town's electricity and gas supplies are shut off. The wind direction away from large population areas is favorable, however as a fire breaks out and intensifies, a mandatory evacuation order is given. No-one is certain when residents will be able to return to their homes or what they will return to.

Do these disaster scenarios seem far-fetched? Do you think they could ever happen to you? Can you guarantee that something similar could *never* happen to you?

Before we continue, let's briefly consider the groups of people who are most vulnerable to disasters:

- **The financially poor** usually lack the means to adequately prepare for a disaster by putting food and other resources aside. When living from day to day, they may be unable to save money and build up reserves to fend for themselves when disaster strikes. This group can include the short and long term unemployed who do not have sufficient cash reserves.

- **The elderly** (65 years or older) face many challenges especially if they are living alone, are physically unable to cope, or have particular medical or nutritional needs. Furthermore, they may be reluctant to request help for fear that it will lead to a loss of independence and possible institutionalization.

- **Pregnant or postpartum women, and the very young** (newborn and infants) may be at risk due to factors such as heightened levels of stress, medical complications, environmental contamination, and disruption of pre- and post-natal care.

- **People with mobility impairments** such as those who depend on wheelchairs and other mobility devices may need help, especially if electrical power has been cut.

- **The deaf and hard of hearing** may be placed at a disadvantage because they are unable to hear warning sirens and important radio or T.V. announcements.

- **The visually impaired and people with service animals** may require special assistance to navigate damaged structures and have help with their possibly distressed animals.

- **People with cognitive disabilities and the mentally ill** may have limited capacity to comprehend or contain the severity of the situation. They are likely to need reassurance and special assistance.

- **People with special medical conditions or dietary needs** may require regular access to important medical supplies, services, or nutritional items.

- **Widows, orphans, one-parent families** and other people lacking supportive relationships may require special assistance.

- **Women and children** may potentially be exposed to risks from trafficking and other abuse. Special protection should be afforded to such people.

- **Children at school or daycare facilities** may require special assistance if there is a disproportionate ratio between themselves and their carers at the time a disaster strikes.

- **People living in substandard housing** such as mobile homes, and poorly constructed or situated dwellings are more likely to be at risk from some types of disaster such as severe weather and flooding.

- **People with little or no insurance** may be left without the financial means to recover from the damage caused by a disaster.

- **People who rely on social welfare** are at risk if they have no other means to provide for their basic needs.

- **People without transportation** could be left stranded unless their need to evacuate is taken into consideration.

- **Non-native language speakers** may be vulnerable if they do not have an adequate grasp of the local language. Their ability to heed important announcements and instructions may put them at risk. Examples include new immigrants, refugees, and foreign tourists.

- **Marginalized groups** consist of people who are on the fringes of society and may be at risk if their needs are not always anticipated or planned for. Some examples include refugees, the homeless, the illiterate, people from religious and ethnic minorities, and others who are considered marginal based on their social standing, gender or sexuality.

Any of these types of people can be vulnerable in a disaster. Perhaps you know people like this? As part of your disaster preparedness planning, think of how you can help vulnerable people within your community.

2. Five Disaster Trends

"I don't set trends.
I just find out what they are and exploit them."
Dick Clark

Due to the increase of reporting and classification of disasters, we are gaining an ever-clearer picture of the nature and trends of disasters.

What is disturbing is that the number of disasters is increasing and despite being statistically less deadly, they are affecting more people and incurring an ever-increasing financial burden on affected and unaffected nations alike.

Globally, we observe the following five trends:

Trend #1: The number of people affected by disasters is rising.
As the population of the world increases, people find themselves having to occupy areas where the prevalence of natural hazards is more common. In our need for food, water, living space and access to commerce, we have assumed that exposure to hazards and risk is an accepted part of life or can be effectively managed. As more people become concentrated together, the hazard risks they face will inevitably increase.

Trend #2: Disasters are becoming less deadly.

The advantages of modern science and an increasing ability to adapt to the natural environment have in part enabled us to predict, avoid, and manage the threat of natural disaster. This is certainly true for the majority of common hazards such as meteorological, hydrological and biological threats. For less common hazards such as earthquakes and hurricanes, there is a lower rate of success, particularly in poorer countries which lack access to the technology and technological expertise afforded to wealthier nations. In the case of nations who are experiencing a decline in the number of fatalities, these changes can be attributed to:

- More organized and comprehensive disaster preparedness campaigns that help individuals and communities decrease their levels of vulnerability.
- Early warning systems that allow potential victims to remove themselves out of harm's way.
- Special protection systems designed to withstand the effects of disaster and protect life (such as tornado-safe rooms).
- Building codes and enforcements increase the resilience of structures and systems on which people depend.
- Proper zoning and enforcements prevent people from living in dangerous areas.

- Sustainable development practices are helping people from having to move into high-risk areas.

Trend #3: Disasters are becoming more costly.

Some of the reasons for this have already been mentioned: increasing population, increasing population density, and a greater number of disasters, etc. People are living in areas where their financial assets (homes, businesses, etc.) are being put at greater risk of financial loss when disaster strikes. Also, economies which are more dependent on technology tend to fail when disaster strikes, thus resulting in greater financial damages.

Trend #4: Poor countries are disproportionately affected by disaster consequences.

Natural disasters strike anywhere and do not differentiate between rich and poor nations. However, developing countries bear the greatest burdens for a variety of reasons including:

- Substandard housing unable to withstand the effects of disasters.
- Tendency for people to live along the coast or on floodplains where storm surges, hurricanes, tsunamis and floods strike.
- Lack of education on issues that could save lives when disaster strikes.

- Lack of appropriate health care to deal with secondary, post-disaster consequences.
- Lack of funding for disaster preparedness and mitigation.

Trend #5: The number of disasters is increasing each year. The number of disasters is on the increase and is unlikely to alter without significant changes in settlement and development practices. An increase in technology and social strife means that man-made disasters are also on the rise.

The conclusion we can draw from these trends is that we must be all the more prepared to deal with the threat of disasters no matter where they occur.

No one can predict exactly what disasters will happen or when they will occur. If this was possible, disasters would probably not exist since we could take the appropriate action to avoid them! What we are certain of is that disasters and emergencies *do* happen and we should take the necessary time and effort to prepare for what is *most likely* to occur since we cannot plan for every eventuality.

3. What is Disaster Preparedness?

*"There's no harm in hoping for the best
as long as you're prepared for the worst."*
— Stephen King, Different Seasons

We talk about *"disaster preparedness"* but what exactly is it? How do we define it?

Disaster preparedness is the process by which you can:

- Maintain a state of readiness to contain the effects of a disaster and to minimize loss of life, injury and damage to property.
- Provide rescue, relief and rehabilitation in the aftermath of a disaster.
- Sustain your well-being without being overwhelmed by the demands placed on you.

Disaster preparedness measures can take many forms. Some are to do with strategically setting aside physical items such as food, water, emergency kits, communications equipment, backup systems and the like, such that there are always supplies on hand when a disaster strikes. Another form is to develop written plans detailing how people might behave in specific situations, for example, follow an evacuation route or meet at a certain location.

Other forms of disaster preparedness are called **mitigation**. These are measures that can be taken to reduce the chance of a disaster occurring in the first place, or reduce the damaging effects of an unavoidable disaster. For example, building flood defenses or clearing combustible material from around your home.

You can also think of disaster preparedness as a form of insurance. Most of us have some type of insurance to protect our concerns. For example:

- Home and contents insurance
- Life and disability insurance
- Loss of income insurance
- Vehicle insurance
- Health insurance
- Financial savings
- Liability insurance
- Identity theft protection

How many of these forms of insurance do you have right now?

Your regular home and contents insurance policy may help you recover from the long-term effects of a disaster caused by a tornado or flood, but in the hours and days following a disaster you cannot expect your insurance company to provide you with food, clean water, emergency shelter, first aid supplies, and everything else needed for your *immediate* survival. This is something *you* need to make happen *now*.

Your disaster preparedness "insurance policy" is one you get to write, decide what the terms are, how much you can afford and when you can start making claims without completing official paperwork! After all, the reason we have insurance is because no one can predict the future or what bad things may happen to us. You would never need insurance if you could be certain that nothing bad will ever happen to you!

Disasters are like any other life-event you hope to avoid. When you're prepared for them you can withstand their effects more easily, speed recovery and be in a position to help others around you. You should therefore ready yourself by setting aside resources that can be called on when the unexpected occurs.

Disaster preparedness puts you in a position of relative strength rather than one of weakness, and if done carefully no form of disaster preparedness is a wasted effort.

4. Why Prepare For a Disaster?

"A prudent man sees danger and takes refuge,
but the simple keep going and suffer for it."
— Proverbs 22:3

The goal of disaster preparedness is to reduce your vulnerability to the effects of a disaster and increase your capacity to survive and thrive in the adverse situation.

Simply stated, *"Prepare **now** so you won't have to suffer the consequences **later!**"*

Have you ever watched scenes on T.V. of people panic buying food and water at the store because of an impending storm? The once full shelves are soon laid bare and the helpless shoppers who arrived too late don't know what to do.

You don't want to be like that!

Here are the most common reasons you need to be prepared:

- Delays in help arriving
- Power outages
- Road closures
- Damage to your property
- Lack of drinking water
- Lack of food

- Limited medical help
- Limited or no communications
- Limited transportation
- Need to relocate to an emergency shelter

In 2016 we experienced a heavy snowstorm in Colorado, USA. The news channels warned us it was coming and very quickly the shops began to run low on basic food supplies.

Did I panic? No.

I've already taken steps to make sure that if any disaster cut off vital food, water, or fuel supplies, my family can keep going for at least four weeks without any outside help.

A few weeks later, a major power line in our neighborhood failed and we lost electricity for over 24 hours. The outside temperature was below freezing and many of our neighbors left to stay at a hotel or to eat out (yes, this was a "first world" emergency!)

Did I panic? No.

I grabbed a nearby flashlight, cranked up our emergency electrical generator, cooked a hot meal on the kitchen gas stove (we also have an electric stove in the basement) and made it a fun experience for the kids. Our house was the only one on the street with lights on, and we could still charge our computers and cell phones. No worries!

Is this paranoia? No, it's good judgement and forward thinking. I don't live in fear but in confidence. I'm confident that because I've taken the time to prepare for unforeseen events such as these, I can ride the storm more easily when it arrives.

The impact of a disaster may be sudden, massive, and have long-term implications. Aside from the potential loss of life and property which is often how disasters are remembered, the impact of such events can be observed in many other ways.

For example, in the days or hours leading up to a potential disaster some of the following may occur:

- Stores quickly run out of essential supplies or shut their doors.
- Roadways become congested with people trying to get home or leave the area.
- Long lines of vehicles waiting to buy fuel.
- Public transit has no emergency plan to evacuate people lacking transportation.
- Places to stay (such as hotels, motels, and campgrounds) outside the disaster zone quickly fill up.
- News and information is inconsistent or misleading.

- Some people deny they are in any danger, while others work hard to minimize the risk.

Immediately following a disaster many of the following physical impacts can be expected. Some impacts are more severe than others, but depending on the nature and severity of the disaster none are entirely unrealistic:

- **Public and Private Buildings**
  o Significant damage to public and private buildings.
  o People are left homeless or without adequate shelter.
  o People become displaced and disoriented.
  o Increased exposure to the elements and disease.
  o Decreased protection from criminal activity.
  o Fires may break out and may be left to burn uncontrolled.

- **Personal Possessions**
  o Loss of useful possessions that could aid immediate survival and long-term recovery. Survivors are sometimes literally left with only the clothes on their backs!

- o Loss of family photos and keepsakes can be a difficult experience, particularly if loved ones have died.

- **Transportation Infrastructure** (vehicles, roads, rail networks, airports, seaports, rivers, tunnels, bridges)
  - o This affects the ability to transport emergency personnel, supplies and recovery materials to affected areas and evacuate victims to safer areas.
  - o The impact may be particularly acute in mountainous or coastal areas where there are few alternative routes.
  - o Damage to key structures such as bridges and tunnels can be expensive and time consuming to fix.
  - o Can place a heavy burden on alternative transportation methods such as helicopters.
  - o The time and cost to get fresh goods to market may increase.

- **Power Infrastructure** (electricity, gas, fuel supplies)
  - o Electricity, gas, and fuel services may be cut-off.
  - o Downed power lines and ruptured fuel lines may pose a safety issue.

- o Mobile electrical generators may become increasingly in demand and scarce and ready access to fuel may become a problem.
- o Alternative means of cooking and heating may become necessary.
- o Reliance on solar power and other alternatives to mains electricity to recharge mobile phones and batteries.
- o Fuel prices may increase sharply with a dwindling supply.

- **Communications Infrastructure** (landlines, cellular phone network, radio towers)
  - o Landline phones may cease to operate.
  - o Cellular communications are likely to be severely affected.
  - o SMS text messaging may offer a viable alternative to voice communications.
  - o Email and web access may be severely limited.
  - o Amateur radio operations will become increasingly important.

- **Public Commerce**
  - o Use of bank ATM machines may be limited or unavailable.
  - o Insistence on "cash only" transactions.

- o Stores may close and many essential goods will become hard to find.
- o The cost of essential goods may increase with possible price gouging by some retailers.
- o Panic buying may lead to shortages of bottled water, basic food items, and fuel.

- **Tools and Machinery**
  - o Damage to repair shops and facilities may hamper recovery.
  - o Opportunists may offer their services or equipment for a fee (e.g. private vehicles as taxis, electrical generators, water pumps, etc.)

- **Public Water Supply**
  - o Restricted access to clean water for drinking, cooking, and cleaning.
  - o Increased reliance on bottled water.
  - o Portable water purification systems will become more important.

- **Waste Removal**
  - o Broken sewer lines leak dirty water into rivers and public places.
  - o Trash buildup attracts vermin and other disease carrying vectors.

- Disposal of trash in an unsafe manner can introduce harmful toxins into the environment.
- Lack of adequate drainage and standing water provides places for mosquitoes to breed.

- **Public Health**
  - Many of the above mentioned impacts can place the health of the affected population at risk.
  - Need to educate the public on basic health and safety measures.
  - Makeshift hospitals and substandard medical environments.
  - Increased burden placed on neighboring medical facilities.
  - Loss of diagnostic equipment, inability to refrigerate medicines, or sterilize surgical equipment.
  - Large numbers of dead bodies.

As you formulate your disaster preparedness plan, think about the effects a disaster would have on your community. You should not expect anything to be "business as usual" and therefore must plan to be as self-sufficient as possible, including providing your own accommodation, drinking water, food, transportation, communications, tools, and general supplies.

Planning is an essential element for success in most walks of life. Disaster preparedness is no exception. In fact, having a workable, tested and effective plan in the unfolding chaos of a disaster can literally make the difference between life and death.

Here are four main reasons why you need a disaster preparedness plan:

1. **To set direction and priorities**. By being clear on *what* needs to be done, *who* needs to do it, *when* it needs to be done by, and most importantly *why* it needs to be done, your plan will create a roadmap for success. The goal of your plan is to ensure your safety and avoid making costly mistakes. Therefore develop your plan and test it out before disaster strikes. That way you won't waste precious time figuring out what to do when the world is collapsing around you. Identifying the relative importance of each task will help ensure you do the most important things first.

2. **To get everyone on the same page**. One goal of your plan is to have everyone agree it is realistic and workable. A plan that does not educate or empower others to take action is ineffective. Your family needs to have a sense of ownership in the plan, so involve everyone in the process. Invite discussion, welcome

different opinions and make it as fun as possible. This may take time as you work out the kinks, but the end result will be a plan that everyone feels they own and can make happen when the time comes.

3. **To simplify decision-making.** When an emergency happens you need a clear mind and a way to make good decisions. Time may be short and you need to act quickly and decisively. If your family members are in different places when disaster strikes and the cell-phone service is down, you need to agree beforehand where you should meet and what contingencies you will have in place. Having a clear, well-conceived and pre-determined plan of action will reduce fear and give everyone a relative sense of security. Your plan will help reduce the likelihood of arguments or the tendency to second guess one another.

4. **To help inform others.** Your plan can become an important teaching tool and a template for others to follow. You should encourage other family members, friends, neighbors and co-workers to make their own disaster preparedness plan. In the event of a disaster isn't it better that other people have their own plan in place than to become a burden on others?

A good disaster preparedness plan is:

- **Something you need to make happen yourself!** You need to be in control of your disaster preparedness plan because ultimately your life may depend on it.
- **Part of your lifestyle.** To some extent, your disaster preparedness plan needs to be woven into your way of thinking, your financial budget, and your day-to-day priorities.
- **Tailored to your specific needs.** A disaster preparedness plan that works for one person may not be right for you. There are general principles to observe, but how you execute your plan is usually determined by your family and community dynamics, climate and geography.
- **Flexible and open to continual improvement.** A disaster preparedness plan cannot be so rigid that it's impossible to change. Your plan must adapt to changing circumstances because disasters by their very definition do not play according to our rules.
- **Something to be shared, taught, and practiced.** A disaster preparedness plan needs to be communicated to others so that it becomes a source of reassurance, and that by practicing it others may gain useful knowledge and skills.

5. Most People Are Not Prepared!

*"Because sometimes things happen to people
and they're not equipped to deal with them."*
— **Suzanne Collins, The Hunger Games: Catching Fire**

Let's face it – most people are not prepared for disasters. There are a wide variety of reasons for this including:

- **Denial** (*"it will never happen to me", "it's someone else's problem, not mine"*)
- **Time and money** (*"I can't afford it", "it's a waste of time and money"*)
- **Lack of community involvement** (*"it's not my responsibility", "the government will help us"*)
- **Lack of knowledge or imagination** (*"I wouldn't know where to start", "I'm just not into all that Doomsday, apocalyptic nonsense!"*)
- **Lack of will** (*"what's the point?", "I'll cross that bridge when the time comes"*)

I said I would try and avoid references to North American disasters, but the following statement is very revealing:

"A recent [April 2015] Federal Emergency Management Agency (FEMA) survey found that nearly 60 percent of American adults have not practiced what to do in a disaster by

participating in a disaster drill or preparedness exercise at work, school, or home in the past year. Further, only 39 percent of respondents have developed an emergency plan and discussed it with their household. This is despite the fact that 80 percent of Americans live in counties that have been hit with a weather-related disaster since 2007."[2]

I suspect this unfortunate tendency towards complacency and the lowering of our guard is probably shared by many other parts of the world.

How about you? Have you become complacent? Have you lowered your guard?

Take the following "Ten Point Preparedness Assessment" to see how disaster prepared you are right now. Give yourself one point for every statement that is true for you:

1. I am aware of the potential disaster risks in my area.
2. I have at least two weeks supply of non-perishable food items in my home.
3. I have at least two weeks supply of drinking water in my home.
4. I never allow my vehicle's gas tank to go less than half-full.

---

[2] www.fema.gov news release HQ-15-019

5. I have completed a basic first aid course within the last eighteen months.

6. I have at least one fire extinguisher in my home and vehicle.

7. I have access to an emergency generator or solar power system.

8. I have two-way radio communications equipment which I'm licensed to use.

9. I carry a printed list of emergency contacts with me at all times.

10. My family has pre-arranged emergency meeting points.

How did you score?

- **If you scored a perfect ten**, that is awesome! But please read on, I'm sure there are more things you can do to improve.
- **If you scored five or more**, you're doing better than most people and that's saying something!
- **If you scored less than three**, you have some work to do. Don't worry, we all had to start somewhere and it doesn't take much effort to quickly improve.

Before we continue, let's take a few moments and set the context for your individual disaster preparedness planning.

Take a sheet of paper and write down your observations for each of the following assessments. These will help you shape your thinking about how your disaster preparedness plan needs to be focused.

1. **Assess your most likely threats.** What types of disaster could happen in your area? If you live in a coastal area it could be tsunamis. In low-lying areas it could be flooding. In mountainous areas it could be snowstorms or mudslides. In an earthquake-prone region of the world you're already quite familiar with the dangers. You cannot be expected to prepare for *every* type of disaster but you should prepare for those *most likely* in your location.

2. **Assess the needs and abilities of yourself and your family.** How physically fit are you? What is your financial capacity to buy preparedness related items? What practical skills or assets do you have? How well connected are you to your community?

3. **Assess the level of preparedness of your neighbors and the wider community.** You probably have an idea of how well prepared your local community is based on past experience and the prevailing economic and social climate. All these factors will contribute towards how well you can survive and thrive following a disaster.

4. **Assess who the vulnerable people in your neighborhood.** Hopefully, as you formulate your disaster preparedness plans you will think about the needs of your neighbors. Do you have an elderly or sick person living close by, a family with a special needs child, a single parent without a car, a family with no reliable source of income, or someone unable to speak the native language? If you're able, try and make provision for people beyond your immediate family circle. Strong communities are essential in post-disaster recovery efforts and that strength will come from people like you working together.

Not knowing where you live, how exposed you are to disaster hazards, or your capacity to make adequate preparations for them, it's impossible for me to tell you exactly how you should prepare. Nevertheless, your answers to these questions will help you think more clearly about how you can be better prepared.

Everyone should cultivate a basic understanding of how to remain safe following a disaster. Such knowledge cannot be left to the responsibility of a few "specialists". When disaster strikes it may be too late to learn these fundamental skills. The best first step is to create a disaster preparedness kit.

6. Disaster Preparedness Kits

"To be prepared is half the victory."
— Miguel de Cervantes

The first 72-hours following a disaster are critical. Three days is the amount of time during which you're more likely to have to fend for yourself. It may take this long for emergency responders to reach you or for the situation to stabilize. During this period you may need to attend to your own medical needs, provide your own drinking water and food, construct a makeshift shelter, keep warm, and gather news about what just happened. Ideally, you should have enough supplies for at least 14 days.

The idea with a 72-hour disaster preparedness kit is to have all the basic survival items in one convenient "ready to use" package such as a plastic tote, backpack, or rolling duffel bag. If you become stranded or need to find your own way home, your kit will provide you with food, shelter and communications. If you need to seek refuge at an emergency shelter, these supplies will provide extra comfort items. Make sure you are able to comfortably carry your kit on foot over some distance if necessary.

My family's disaster preparedness kits consist of a few canvas bags we keep on a shelf in the garage. If we ever need to evacuate, we will throw them into the back of one of our vehicles and go! I also keep a personal 72-hour kit in my truck. We store all the emergency water, food and other preparedness supplies in a separate area in our house. Everything has its own place and we don't confuse day-to-day items with those strictly reserved *"for emergencies only."* Store your kits in an easily accessible place such as an entrance way closet or in the garage.

The maxim, *"two is one and one is none"* is often heard within military and preparedness circles. It transforms the somewhat fatalistic saying, *"whatever can go wrong, will go wrong"* into something you can actually do something about. It's all about making sure you have a backup in place should your first line of defense fail for whatever reason. As you gather your disaster preparedness items, think about what might happen if the item failed and what you could use as a substitute.

For example, if your only light source is a flashlight that depends on batteries, what will you do when the batteries run out? If you have no backup or contingency in place, you will literally be left in the dark! An effective fallback might be to pack a hand-crank operated flashlight or several glow sticks. Likewise, to start a fire, don't rely only on matches that may get wet — pack a reliable lighter and fire-striker as well.

Think of these fallback items as extra layers of protection, which will increase your advantage over future adversity. Without them your preparedness efforts may count for nothing.

I will present many of the items needed for your disaster preparedness kit later in the book, but for your convenience here is a checklist of 30 of the most important items you should have. It's not an exhaustive list and I have not included drinking water or food, so you will obviously need to add those too!

#	Item	✔
1	First aid kit	
2	First aid manual	
3	Battery powered radio	
4	Flashlights	
5	Spare batteries	
6	Large tarpaulin sheet	
7	Paracord	
8	Water purification tablets	
9	Water filter	
10	Water containers	
11	Toilet paper	
12	Hand sanitizer	
13	Wet wipes	
14	Trash bags	

15	Duct tape	
16	Dust masks	
17	Work gloves	
18	Safety goggles	
19	Pry bar	
20	Multifunction tool	
21	Notepad and pencil	
22	Whistle	
23	Candles	
24	Matches	
25	Glow sticks	
26	Mylar blankets	
27	Sleeping bag or blanket	
28	Extra clothing	
29	Games and reading material	
30	Emergency contact list	

Discover more 72-hour kit ideas at:

www.disaster.zone/resource/72hourkits

Now that we've laid the groundwork, let's get familiar with the practical nuts and bolts of disaster preparedness by looking at 100 steps you can start today...

Earthquake disaster response, Haiti

7. Your Health and Social Well-Being

"Health is not valued until sickness comes."

— Thomas Fuller

What ultimately determines your ability to survive a disaster, both in the short- and long-term, may not be your raw physical strength or the array of disaster preparedness items you've accumulated, but by your mental and emotional aptitude, and by how well connected you are to others in your community. For example, single parents may be at a higher risk of developing psychiatric problems after a disaster since they often have fewer resources to begin with. Any fragile social connections can be lost after a disaster, thus leading to greater distress.

Your capacity to cope with the negative effects of adversity can be built up and reinforced through positive learning experiences, and by the efforts of individuals and communities working together through adversity.

When we talk about reducing our vulnerability to a disaster, we need to think about how to increase our resilience. The goal of this section is to consider some of the ways you can build up your resilience to the effects of hardship.

1. **Remind yourself that you're not infallible.** Everyone has their limitations and no-one is immune from harm. Make an honest assessment of the physical, mental, emotional and social limitations for each member of your family. Your disaster preparedness plan needs to bring all these factors into careful consideration.

2. **Be physically fit and healthy.** People who have a greater level of physical and mental fitness are more likely to withstand the stresses brought on by a disaster. For you it may mean losing weight by taking regular daily exercise and eating healthier foods, cutting back on alcohol, or to quit smoking. Whatever it is, seek the advice of a medical professional to formulate a plan to get you on the road to being healthier. Furthermore, get an annual medical checkup to stay on track and catch problems early.

3. **Learn something new every day.** Develop the practice of acquiring some new knowledge everyday by studying an educational article or online how-to video. Perhaps take up a new hobby. This will serve to keep your brain active and in a condition where fresh ideas and thoughts can help to construct new ones. Your ability to think through problems and devise alternative solutions can be a huge asset in the face of disaster. Your mind is like a

muscle, if you don't exercise it frequently, it will fall into atrophy and lose its effectiveness.

4. **Simplify your stuff.** Selling the possessions you don't need will help declutter your living space and make extra cash for other things (including building up your disaster preparedness supplies!) Decluttering your lifestyle can help you maintain a more relaxed grip on life and remind you that your true worth is more than the stuff you own.

5. **Get to know your neighbors.** Following a disaster, your immediate neighbors will most likely be the "first responders" to come to your aid. They will not always have the specialized training or equipment that your local emergency services possess (who will most likely be overwhelmed with the unfolding crises), but your neighbors may be the first and possibly only people to come to your aid. Now is the time to build bridges with the people in your neighborhood.

6. **Increase your social circle by making new friends.** And I'm not talking about social media "friends"! I mean people you get to know by having actual face-to-face conversations. By taking the time to appreciate others and being appreciated in return you're building up a valuable asset which is like money in the bank. You can

share this social capital when times get tough. Some practical suggestions include joining a local church, meetup group, sports club, or attending an adult education class.

7. **Add your favorite reading materials, card games, puzzle books, children's toys, etc.** to your 72-hour kits. Following a disaster, being able to take your mind of things for a while and help pass the time can help ease the stress. These items will provide tremendous psychological benefits as well icebreakers to connect with others in a public emergency shelter. A personal media player preloaded with your favorite music or shows can also be a source of mental comfort, but don't forget to use headphones to avoid irritating people nearby who may not share your taste in entertainment!

Discover more disaster health ideas at:

www.disaster.zone/resource/health

8. Be Aware of Your Surroundings

"You can observe a lot by watching."

— Yogi Berra

Some surprises are welcome, others are not. Being able to look ahead and identify potential threats will help you steer clear of them. Heeding the warnings of others and listening to your instincts could literally save your life.

8. **Learn about the different types of disaster hazards** that exist in your area. Is there a nuclear power plant near you, or a busy rail line that carries toxic materials? Mark potential hazards on a local map and discuss with your family or coworkers what steps you would take to minimize the risk or how to escape the danger they present.

9. **Pay attention to the weather forecast.** Install a weather app on your phone that can alert you of approaching bad weather events. Alternatively, find out if you can get email or text message alerts for your area. Subscribing to several methods of early warning will increase your chances of hearing about a danger sooner than later.

10. **Practice taking the stairs to exit your work-place instead of the elevator.** Do you know where all the emergency exits are? Would you be able to help other people find these exits in an emergency? Whenever I stay at a hotel, I first locate the emergency exit stairs after I check in to my room and then navigate the route to the hotel exit. This way I know which way I should exit in an emergency. I also request a room well below the 8th floor. Most fire truck ladders can only reach the 8th-10th floors of high rise buildings!

11. **Identify safe locations where you will meet your family members** if you get separated and lose communications. Identify places within your immediate neighborhood, within your town, and on the outskirts of town. Write these "meeting places" down and make sure each family member has their own copy (see the worksheet at the end of the book.) Each of my family members has a laminated card that lists the different meeting places, important contact names and phone numbers. Visit each location as a family group and discuss their importance.

Discover more disaster awareness ideas at:
www.disaster.zone/resource/awareness

9. What to Carry Every Day

"Her mother always said that
dressing properly could save one's life."
— Susana Fortes

People in the disaster preparedness community refer to the things we carry each day as our "EDC" (Every Day Carry) items or kit. These are items that will become useful to us in a disaster situation when no other emergency items are at hand. Many of the items mentioned in this book could quite easily be included in your EDC kit, so this section isn't an exhaustive list.

12. **Dress for the weather** and not your office or vehicle. Choose layers of comfortable clothing with functional pockets and a belt. Avoid wearing cotton if possible, especially in cold or wet conditions. Wet cotton clothing will sap the heat from your body and takes longer to dry. Wear comfortable shoes or keep a pair at the ready in your office or vehicle. Pack an extra warm layer, a jacket or coat, hat and gloves in your backpack. If you're left stranded and have to walk some distance you'll be glad you had the extra clothing and footwear.

13. **Use a small day pack to carry your extra items.** It doesn't have to be conspicuous or bulky — just something sensible. Add a water bottle and a few energy

bars, but save these for when you really need them. A few other items worth carrying include a rain poncho, local street map, compass, flashlight, notepad and pencil.

14. **Carry some form of photo ID** preferably with your home address on it. If you ever need to get through a road block to reach your house, proof of where you live will be very helpful. Some governments issue credit-card sized "Passport Cards" which in some circumstances could potentially be used to pass through international borders.

15. **Carry an amount of cash** enough to get a bus or taxi home. Keep small denominations so that you'll never have to pay more than is necessary if no change is available.

16. **Always carry your keys with you** in case you need them in a hurry. For example, never leave them on your desk at work if you're in a meeting in another part of the building. If you have to leave without any time to spare, you'll be glad you were able to access your vehicle for shelter or to evacuate the area.

17. **A small LED flashlight** on your key-ring takes up very little space and can be very useful during a power cut.

18. **Keep a few adhesive bandages in your wallet, purse or daypack.** If you cannot carry a full first aid kit, having a few of these will help with minor cuts and abrasions.

19. **A small book of matches or a lighter** may come in handy if you need to start a fire for warmth or signaling. Keep them dry in a sealed plastic bag and make sure you learn the art of starting a fire with only one match.

20. **Carry a small pocket knife or multi-tool.** Knives have so many uses and especially in an emergency when you may need to cut through a seat-belt or to free trapped clothing. If it isn't practical to carry a knife that may be visible to others, there are many flat "credit card" sized knives available that can be concealed within a wallet.

Discover more disaster EDC ideas at:

www.disaster.zone/resource/edc

10. Water, Sanitation and Hygiene

"We never know the worth of water, till the well is dry."

— **Thomas Fuller**

Life simply cannot exist without water, so you must give it the highest consideration in your disaster preparedness planning. If you had to shelter in your home for an extended period of time, how long could you and your family survive if the water supply to your house had been cut off due to a ruptured pipe or widespread contamination? You could probably survive for a few days by finding some bottled water in your cupboards, taking water from the hot and cold plumbing pipes, melting ice from the freezer, and by collecting some rain water, but could you find enough for more than a few days, or even weeks? Other disaster preparedness categories pale to insignificance when compared to our fundamental need for water.

You should ensure an **absolute minimum** supply of four liters (one gallon) of water per person per day for drinking and minimal hygiene and have at least a seven day supply set aside. For a family of four people that quickly adds up to a lot of water per week (112 liters, or about 30 gallons). Ideally, you should have at least a two week supply.

Did you know that one of the greatest causes of death following a disaster can be attributed to water-borne disease due to contaminated water, including dysentery, hepatitis A, viral gastroenteritis, typhoid, and diphtheria? Your supplies must therefore include items to help maintain adequate levels of hygiene and sanitation.

Following the 2010 earthquake in Haiti, many people who survived the initial disaster became ill due to cholera. The disease quickly spread and by August 2015 it had affected some 754,000 people and killed over 9,000. In response to this crisis, my non-profit organization worked with other disaster relief groups to install large water purification units in several camps housing several hundred earthquake survivors. I am certain that because of this proactive intervention we were able to save many lives. Another simple, yet effective measure we introduced was to use old oil drums as waste collection points around the camps. We painted them in bright colors to encourage people to put their litter in the drums instead of on the ground.

Your disaster preparedness plan must look at how you can store an adequate supply of water, how you can make it safe to drink, how you can conserve the water you have and what basic steps you can take for basic sanitation and hygiene.

21. **Store a large supply of commercially available bottled water.** Bottled water is a safe and reliable source of drinking water in an emergency. Because bottled

water is packaged as a food product under strictly controlled sanitary conditions and does not contain substances such as proteins and sugars typically associated with food spoilage, it can be stored indefinitely as long as it remains unopened in a cool, dark place. You can safely ignore the sell-by date on packaged bottled drinking water. On the downside, bottled water is expensive and generally cost-prohibitive for stockpiling large volumes. Even so, the convenience factor should not be overlooked when you can easily distribute and carry several bottles of safe, potable water in your vehicle or 72-hour kit. You should therefore include bottled water as part of your disaster preparedness plan. Do not use milk or juice containers for long-term water storage. The milk protein and fruit sugars cannot be adequately removed from these containers and will provide an environment for bacteria to grow and spoil the water.

22. **A 55 gallon (208 liter) water barrel** can store a large volume of emergency water in your basement or garage. 55 gallons is enough to supply a family of four for about two weeks (1 gallon/day x 4 people x 14 days = 56 gallons). Make sure the airtight barrel is designed to store potable water for extended periods of time and has

not been used to store anything else. If your regular tap water is treated, there's no need to add special chemicals prior to storing it. Otherwise you can treat the water just before using it. Store the barrel in a cool, dark place where it can be easily drained and refilled at least once a year. Use a siphon to get the water out of the barrel for day to day use.

23. **Get a container of plain, unscented household bleach** (containing 5% sodium hypochlorite) to treat your drinking water. Add 2 drops of bleach to each liter of water (8 drops per gallon), stir well and allow to stand for 30 minutes. If the water has a slight chlorine smell it's safe to drink. A stronger bleach solution can also be used to clean dishes and other surfaces used for food preparation.

24. **Get a supply of water purification tablets.** Common internationally recognized brands are *Puritabs* and *Aquatabs*. These are a convenient, though more expensive, way to treat smaller volumes of water. They are usually available from camping suppliers and online retailers.

25. **Add a portable water filter**. The filtration device should have at least a 0.2 micron pore size. This is the largest

diameter hole in the filter designed to prevent the passage of harmful pathogens. The smaller the pore size the better. You can use regular paper coffee filters to remove larger suspended solids from your source water before using the water filter.

26. **Add some sturdy water containers with airtight seals.** For the purposes of hygiene and convenience it is a good idea for each person in your household to have their own personal water bottle. Write each person's name on their container to avoid any confusion.

27. **Don't overlook the water needs of your pets and animals.** Allocate the same amount for pets as people, that is, one gallon per day. Pack bowls and separate containers to store their water.

28. **Set aside basic hygiene supplies** such as toilet paper, soap, shampoo, hand sanitizer (60% alcohol based), toothbrushes, toothpaste, dental floss, deodorant, feminine products, comb or hairbrush, disposable razors and babies diapers. These items are important not only for basic hygiene but for providing personal comfort and a sense of well-being. Add a supply of various sized trash bags to help contain and manage waste.

29. **Unscented wet wipes** are really convenient for washing hands and faces, wiping up small messes, keeping cool on a hot day and as an alternative to toilet paper. Wet toilet paper falls apart and becomes useless, but wet wipes will remain functional since they are made from a stronger, fabric-like material.

30. **A simple makeshift toilet** can be constructed from a round five gallon bucket with a lid, a length of foam tubing and a few trash bags. A trash bag is placed around the rim of the bucket and secured in place by the foam tubing that doubles as a crude but functional seat. A toilet roll can be secured through the bucket's handle. Spread scented cat litter or earth over your "business" to mask the smell and place the lid over the seat when not using the toilet. Before use as a toilet, the bucket can be used to contain many disaster supplies and would be ideal for keeping in your vehicle or designated shelter-in-place room.

Discover more disaster water ideas at:

www.disaster.zone/resource/water

11. Food and Meal Preparation

"So long as you have food in your mouth,
you have solved all questions for the time being."

— Franz Kafka

Following a disaster it is essential you're able to enjoy nutritious meals despite the possibility of being unable to obtain certain types of food or familiar brands. You may not be able to find fresh fruit, vegetables or meat, and very quickly your mealtimes may start to resemble a camping trip as you eat out of cans and packets, or wait your turn in an emergency shelter food-line.

Your body and mind will likely experience unfamiliar levels of stress, but a tasty and nutritious meal will deliver a positive physical and morale-giving boost. Your goal should be to have at least two to four weeks supply of food beyond what you would normally keep in your home, but an **absolute minimum** is to have enough for three days.

31. **Stock up on staples** such as rice, noodles, crackers, tuna fish, canned goods (meat, fruit and vegetables), peanut butter, cooking oil, oatmeal, protein and granola bars, nuts, dried fruit, raisins, flour, honey, sugar, tea, coffee, salt, seasonings, etc. Choose food items that have a long shelf life and store them in airtight containers. Dried milk and egg powder are a good option. You should plan for at

least 2,000-3,000 calories a day per person. Rotate your food items, so that you consume the older stock first and replace them with newly purchased supplies when you go shopping. A reasonable goal is to keep a 30 day supply in your home made up largely of non-perishable items. If everyone adopted this preparedness mindset, scenes of panic-buying would be a thing of the past. A three day supply of food for your vehicle or workplace disaster kit is easily manageable.

32. **Pay attention to any special dietary needs your family members may have**, especially infants and toddlers, pregnant and breastfeeding women, diabetics and the elderly. An emergency is not the time to experiment with unfamiliar food items, so avoid stocking up on freeze-dried rations or brands you've never tried before. If in doubt, try a small sample before buying a larger amount. Apart from its nutritional value, food becomes an important psychological boost in a stressful disaster situation. Try and stick with food you know and love that can be stored long-term without spoiling. Also, include some multivitamins and other dietary supplements.

33. **Buy a few items of *"for emergencies only"* food each time you go shopping.** If stored carefully, canned foods

will last well beyond their advertised expiry date. Many canned foods contain liquids that can be an important source of hydration if no potable water is available. Make sure you include meals which require no water to be added or can be eaten without the need for cooking. Avoid salty foods which are likely to increase thirst.

34. **Pack a manual can opener** because opening a can with a rock isn't easy! Some canned foods are equipped with easy-open ring pulls making it convenient to open them by hand. The containers themselves can be used as impromptu cooking pots and dishes if nothing else is available.

35. **Buy a portable propane or butane gas stove.** These are readily available from camping stores and offer a safe and convenient way to heat water or food with minimal effort. Buy an extra propane tank for your barbeque grill and make sure you always have at least one full.

36. **Add a few lightweight cooking pots with lids.** You'll need at least one fairly large pot for boiling drinking water. Aluminum kitchen foil can also be used to cook some food items in an open fire or to protect food from insects.

37. **Get a supply of disposable cups, plates, bowls, knives, forks, spoons and napkins.** If you're short on water to wash your dishes, these disposable items will be invaluable. Otherwise, pack a set of sturdy eating utensils for each person in your family. If you have enough water to wash dishes, add a small amount of bleach to the final rinse water.

38. **Resealable plastic food grade bags** can be used to keep food items fresh and reduce spoilage. You can also use these bags to warm food in hot water and then use the water for making drinks or for washing.

39. **Add a supply of trash bags** to dispose of waste. Trash should eventually be burned or buried and not left in the open to attract the attention of insects and vermin.

Discover more disaster food ideas at:

www.disaster.zone/resource/food

12. Protection and Warmth

"What do you actually need? Food, clothing and shelter.
Everything else is entertainment."

— Aloe Blacc

Protection from the weather and the ability to have a good night's sleep are crucial to surviving a disaster.

Two weeks after the 2010 earthquake in Haiti, the landscape had become a patchwork of blue tarps and tents. There were not enough tents to go around and the few I took with me were quickly snatched up. Sadly, on a second trip to the capital city six months later, I saw many more people continuing to live rough without adequate shelter.

40. **Get a good quality tent.** Since a tent may become your primary refuge following a disaster its best not to go cheap. For comfort, get a tent that can sleep twice the number of people than are in your family. Find tents that have at least the following features: "three-season" rating (can be used spring, summer and fall), sewn-in waterproof "bathtub" floor, full rainfly that covers all sides and extends down to the ground, heavy-duty zippers, mosquito screen doors, roof vents (to promote good airflow), guy ropes and tie-down loops. The ability to store your gear and cook within the tent can be an

advantage in bad weather. For this reason, a tent that has a roomy vestibule is beneficial.

41. **Get some high quality tarpaulin sheets** of different sizes with reinforced grommet holes. "Tarps" as they're often called are frequently used to create an emergency shelter, a temporary privacy wall or to serve as a protective groundsheet. They can also be used to make an impromptu stretcher, a rain poncho or a simple "Yukon" pack.

42. **Get a quality sleeping bag.** Since your sleeping bag will be the primary method of keeping warm at night you should get a bag that is designed for outdoor conditions during the coldest part of the year. Your sleeping bag will likely be one of the more expensive items in your disaster kit. Choosing a bag that minimizes size and weight will cost more but will allow you to pack more items or carry a smaller and lighter disaster preparedness kit. Remember to protect your sleeping bag within at least two layers of plastic such as heavy duty trash bags. During a training exercise in the unforgiving mountains of the Welsh Brecon Beacons, one member of our team neglected this simple precaution and endured several uncomfortable nights shivering in his tent after discovering his sleeping bag was soaked

through from the driving rain. As a general rule, wrap everything in plastic, especially your sleeping and clothing items that cannot be easily dried out.

43. **Insulated sleeping pads** provide two benefits. The first and most important benefit is to provide thermal insulation from the cold ground. The second benefit is to provide a comfortable cushion beneath your body. Your option for an insulated sleeping pad might include an air mattress, air pad, foam pad, or a self-inflating pad. Another option is to use a thick wool blanket.

44. **Include several "space" or "emergency" blankets.** These thin, waterproof, windproof and heat-reflective Mylar™ sheets are designed to reduce a loss of body heat due to thermal radiation, water evaporation, or convection. The silver or gold colored coating on the plastic sheet reflects up to 97% of radiated heat. They are inexpensive, lightweight and compact and should be included in every disaster supplies kit. An additional benefit is that they can be used as an impromptu signaling device.

45. **Pack at least two or three changes of clothing.** If you find yourself in an emergency shelter with no laundry facilities, you'll be glad that you packed some clean

clothes in your disaster preparedness kit. My recommendation is to pack clothes made from quick drying synthetic materials such as nylon and polyester. Place each complete change of clothing in a plastic bag to keep it dry. Don't forget a warm hat, gloves, underwear, socks and clothes to wear at night.

46. **Get a pet carrier or crate.** If you need to evacuate your home and are able to take your pets, having a way to transport them safely is important. Don't forget to pack enough bedding, and a spare collar and leash if you have a dog.

47. **Ear plugs** are great if you share space with noisy sleepers. If *you* are the noisy sleeper, offer them to your companions! Anything that contributes to a good night's sleep for everyone is a benefit to all!

Discover more disaster protection ideas at:

www.disaster.zone/resource/protection

At this point we're about halfway through our list of 100 practical disaster preparedness steps.

You might be thinking that this all sounds like too much work, too much like preparing for a camping trip (which is not everyone's idea of fun), or maybe you thought it would actually be more complicated than this.

A good approach to completing your disaster preparedness is to establish one layer at a time. Start with the foundational layers of water, food and shelter, and then add more layers, which we will now examine.

Emergency response training, Costa Rica

13. First Aid Essentials

"In nothing do men more nearly approach the gods than in giving health to men."

— Cicero

Remember, one definition of a disaster is *"any event that overwhelms existing resources to deal with that event, resulting in widespread destruction and distress."* Given this fact, the only medical help that may be available is that which you provide for yourself. This is a potentially frightening prospect, particularly if the injury is severe. Therefore, preparations should not be taken lightly.

48. **Take a basic first aid course.** It will teach you many valuable skills including how to treat minor wounds, burns, strains, sprains, and basic CPR techniques. Find out when your local Red Cross or Red Crescent office has such courses. They are usually very affordable and will give you the confidence to know how to care for someone when injury strikes... because it could happen at any time!

49. **Buy a basic first aid kit for your home, vehicle and workplace.** Having only one first aid kit is not enough — you'll need at least one kit for each place you spend a lot of time. There are many pre-made "starter" kits available

that contain all the basic supplies you need, including bandages, gauze pads, dressings, disposable gloves, tape, scissors, tweezers and usually a basic first aid guide. You should then supplement these kits with additional items and medicines to suit your individual needs.

50. **Add medications to your kit for treating common ailments.** Be sure to consult a physician if you have concerns about any medications. For **allergic reactions** (epinephrine autoinjector, diphenhydramine, cetirizine, promethazine), **painkillers and anti-inflammatories** (aspirin, acetaminophen, ibuprofen, codeine, aceclofenac, diclofenac), **symptomatic relief** (antidiarrheals, antiemetics, antacids, laxatives, oral rehydration solution, decongestants, cough suppressants or expectorants, cough and throat lozenges, cold and flu remedies, sleeping aids, eye drops, saline nasal sprays, activated charcoal) and **topical medication** (antiseptics and disinfectants, antibiotic ointments, antifungal cream, hydrocortisone cream, burn relief gel, calamine or zinc oxide lotion, compound tincture of benzoin, benzoin tincture plain topical). Include bug spray (containing at least 40% DEET) and sunscreen (at least SPF-30).

51. **Buy a comprehensive first aid manual.** A good manual will go into more detail than your first aid course is likely

to cover. Take the time to study it and keep it close to your first aid kit. If you have a smartphone, you should definitely download the American Red Cross "First Aid" app which provides instant access to information on handling the most common first aid emergencies and will work without an internet connection.

52. **Let everyone in your family know where the first aid kits are kept.** Ideal locations are the kitchen, bathroom, or workshop — in fact any place that is likely to see an injury. Keep the kit inside a clear, airtight plastic box which will help protect it from dust and moisture damage.

53. **Reserve a minimum thirty-day supply of prescription medicines** to deal with any serious existing medical conditions. Talk to your doctor and explain why you believe this is important as part of your disaster preparedness planning. A worksheet for recording important medications and allergies is provided at the end of the book.

Discover more disaster first aid ideas at:
www.disaster.zone/resource/firstaid

14. Power, Fire, and Heat

"The biggest thing that concerns me is when we start getting countries using cybercrime to shut down infrastructure, electricity, communications systems, the Internet, etc."

— **Frank Abagnale**

Can you imagine a world without electricity? No lights, no cell phones, T.V. or radio? Can you imagine not being able to prepare a hot drink, cook a meal, or feel the warmth of a fire on a cold evening?

Your ability to provide all these essential functions becomes crucial following a disaster.

54. **Choose your electronic devices such as radios and flashlights** according to the size of battery they take (usually 1.5V AA or AAA). By standardizing on one or two sizes of battery for all your electronics, you can conveniently share a pool of batteries between all devices without worrying about running out of one particular size and having no replacements. Stock up on batteries and add a cheap voltmeter to test their usefulness before throwing any away. Most good quality batteries can be stored for five to ten years in a cool, dry climate without losing their charge.

55. **Invest in a portable electrical generator.** This is an expensive item but will prove invaluable during a prolonged power outage. Your choice of generator will determine the types of appliances you can operate. For example, a standard refrigerator or washing machine may require as much as 1,800 watts to start up and keep running (the stated wattage multiplied by 1½). A 1,000 watt generator is enough to power a small microwave oven, TV, laptop computer and several 60W lamps but not all at the same time! Follow the correct safety procedures when operating petrol (gasoline) powered generators and never use them in confined spaces or indoors.

56. **Store several gallons of extra fuel** for your electric generator or vehicle, to be used only in emergencies. The highly flammable fuel must be stored in an approved container and preferably in a building away from your main living space. Make sure you use a funnel to safely transfer the fuel without spills.

57. **A solar panel, charge controller, car battery and an inverter** is a convenient way to keep your laptop computers and radio equipment operating. My family has at least one 100-watt solar panel we can take with us anywhere to charge a spare car battery for basic needs.

58. **Get a few items to start a fire for heat or cooking.** For example, a few boxes of matches, some inexpensive cigarette lighters and a magnesium fire starter. There are many ways you can start a fire, some are very straightforward and others involve some skill and practice. Aim to have at least three reliable methods that work for you and make sure you keep your fire-starting items dry.

59. **Add some candles** to your disaster supplies. Small "tea light" candles are very inexpensive and can even be used to help keep metal containers with food and liquids warm. Never leave a burning candle unattended or near flammable materials.

60. **Add a few glow sticks** to your kit. Glow sticks can safely be given to young children for reassuring "comfort" light at night. They come in a variety of colors, are inexpensive, and can also be used to indicate the entrance to a shelter, attract the attention of a search party at night, or mark the location of an injured person.

61. **Equip your home, vehicles and your workplace with fire extinguishers.** Position at least one extinguisher on every floor of your home. Learn how to put out small fires using the P.A.S.S. method (**Pull** the pin, **Aim** low at

the base of the fire, **Squeeze** the handle and then **Sweep** from side to side at the base of the fire until it is out). Equip your home with smoke detectors on every floor and place carbon monoxide (CO) detectors near open flames and gas heaters.

62. **Know how to shut-off the water, electricity and gas to your home.** Following a disaster you will want to protect your home by shutting off these utilities. Many fires are started post-disaster because of ruptured gas lines.

Discover more power, fire, and heat ideas at:

www.disaster.zone/resource/power

15. Communications

"Communication is at the very core of our society.

That's what makes us human."

— Jan Koum

Your ability to gather timely news and communicate effectively with others is probably the most valuable asset after the basic needs for water, food and shelter have been met.

If the Internet, landline and cell phone networks all fail, the only remaining option is traditional "over the airwaves" radio. Unfortunately, not all the options for two-way radio communications described in this section are legal everywhere, sometimes due to stringent laws or because their use is linked to anti-government groups. Exercise the appropriate level of caution if you choose these modes of communication. Other forms of communications are more low-tech and accessible.

63. **A plastic whistle** is an inexpensive and reliable way to attract attention with minimal effort by allowing its shrill sound to be carried much farther than your voice. Most whistles have the means to be tied to a string or lanyard and a brightly colored whistle will be more easily found in low light conditions. Avoid metal whistles that could stick to your lips in very cold weather. Three blasts of a whistle (or flashlight, car horn, firearm, etc.) in close

succession followed by a one-minute pause is an internationally recognized distress signal.

64. **Paper and pen** can be used to leave messages to convey a change of plans, the location of other family members, or an important phone number. Messages should be written in bold block letters, not in cursive which some people may have difficulty reading. To protect the message from the weather, place the paper in a clear, sealable, plastic bag and use strong tape or zip-ties to secure it to an easily noticed surface. Alternatively, *"all-weather"* paper and pens designed for use in most weather conditions are commercially available and can function equally well. Use a permanent marker pen to write messages on walls and other smooth surfaces. A wide-tipped, bold colored marker pen with quick-drying, water-resistant ink will leave a permanent, high-contrast mark that will endure the weather.

65. **Get a high quality battery operated AM/FM radio** for your home and office. In the event of a disaster, the authorities will use local radio to broadcast information including shelter-in-place or evacuation orders, water restrictions, and other emergency related notices. If you decide to get a radio that uses a hand-crank to generate its power, be aware that the crank mechanism is not

failsafe — the handle could break due to overuse and may become tiresome to operate for extended periods of time.

66. **Purchase a weather alert radio.** Besides the usual AM/FM bands, some radios are equipped with special channels to notify you of weather hazards and other types of emergency alerts in your area. Don't forget to pack some headphones to listen to the news when others are sleeping or if you need to conceal potentially distressing news from young children.

67. **Buy a pair of "bubble pack" walkie-talkie radios.** FRS ("Family Radio Service") or GMRS ("General Mobile Radio Service") radios are very handy for short distance communications (less than 1km or about ½ mile) or between vehicles travelling together. Many units are relatively inexpensive and durable if treated with care. However, don't believe the advertised *"15-30 mile range"* you often see with these radios. This is a theoretical range in optimal conditions and has very little bearing on reality. Write down a list of the channels your family will agree to use in a disaster and the times you will check-in on each other, for example *"channel 5 every 30 minutes."* A CB ("Citizens Band") radio is another viable two-way radio communication option. With their extended power

and larger antennas, they have a greater range than FRS/GMRS radios (about 1.6-16 km or 1-10 miles).

68. **Amateur ("ham") radio** is the de facto standard for disaster preparedness and emergency communications. These radios have ranges of several to hundreds or thousands of miles. It's a myth that to become an amateur radio operator is technically difficult or expensive. There are many excellent study guides available that walk you through everything you need to know and the test can usually be passed after 8-12 hours of study. Many inexpensive and reasonably well-made Chinese radios covering popular amateur bands are available through popular online retailers. It is very possible to study for, take the exam and purchase a basic radio for less than US$100. In most countries you're required to have a license to operate amateur and GMRS radios, but in a true disaster situation their use is generally permitted by unlicensed operators where normal communications systems are overloaded, damaged, or disrupted.

69. **A scanner capable of monitoring emergency services** is a particularly useful piece of kit. These radios are often expensive and require knowledge of the types of radio system and frequencies used in your area. Most scanners

are able to tune in to amateur radio bands, air traffic control, railroads, weather information, and public AM and FM stations.

Discover more disaster communication ideas at:

www.disaster.zone/resource/communication

Emergency food distribution to flood victims, India

16. Cell Phones

"My cell phone is my best friend.
It's my lifeline to the outside world."
— Carrie Underwood

According to the International Telecommunications Union (ITU), there are over five billion wireless subscribers; over 70% of them reside in low- and middle- income countries and over 85% of the world's population has wireless signal cover. The modern, ubiquitous cell phone does more than just make voice calls. Many have a built-in GPS, compass, flashlight, and camera. Without a doubt, your cell phone may be the most useful piece of technology available to you in a disaster, which is why I've dedicated an entire section to this topic. Take full advantage of the features your cell phone has to offer.

70. **Carry your phone with you every day.** It's almost redundant to say this given that many people have their faces continually in their phones! Nevertheless, your phone may become the only link you will have with the outside world following a disaster. Many victims of the 2010 Haitian earthquake were located and saved because they were able to send SMS text messages from within collapsed buildings.

71. **Keep your cell phone charged.** Get extra chargers for your home, vehicle and office and keep your phone plugged in to maintain maximum charge. Disable all non-essential, power-hungry functions such as GPS, Bluetooth and Wi-Fi until they're required. Saving your phone's power now will mean you'll have more for when it's really needed.

72. **Install software to maximize your phone battery.** There are many free apps that can help minimize your phone's power usage. Other apps worth adding include first aid guides, weather alerts, emergency service radio scanners, and the "EchoLink" app if you're a licensed amateur radio operator.

73. **Pre-load your phone with all your important contact details** and keep a printed copy of the same details in your wallet or purse (see the worksheet at the end of the book). This list should include a few out-of-state contacts such as a relatives or trusted friends who can act as a go-between to relay important messages. During an emergency local phone circuits may become congested and an out-of-state phone number may be your only opportunity to let others know what's going on. Get permission from these people and let them know how

they can become an important part of your emergency communications plan.

74. **Add "I.C.E." numbers to your contacts list.** I.C.E. is an acronym for "In Case of Emergency" and first responders may try to locate this number on your phone to find out who they can call if you're incapacitated. Create as many I.C.E. contacts as you think are necessary and let each person know you have designated them as an emergency contact.

75. **Protect your phone with a rugged hard-shell case.** Since your phone is an important link to the outside world you should protect it from damage. It could only take one drop on a hard surface to shatter the screen or render the phone unusable. If you're like me, I often carry my phone in my back pocket or shirt pocket. I want to know that it's protected against accidental knocks and drops.

Discover more disaster cell phone ideas at:

www.disaster.zone/resource/cellphones

17. Vehicles and Transportation

"Everything in life is somewhere else,

and you get there in a car."

— Elwyn Brooks White

We have become very reliant upon our motorized vehicles. If you ever need to make a quick escape from an oncoming threat, you will need a reliable form of transportation.

76. **Safety first!** One of the governing mantras in disaster response is, *"don't become a victim yourself."* Practice this when driving by keeping your head and your hands in control of the vehicle at all times. This is a polite way of saying don't drive under the influence of alcohol or drugs, or use your phone! Always wear your seatbelt because it will probably do more to save your life in a vehicle accident that any other safety device. Make sure everyone else in your vehicle is wearing their seatbelt too!

77. **Keep your vehicle well maintained.** Good preventative maintenance is better than a breakdown or hefty repair bill, so make sure to schedule regular check-ups such as oil and fluid changes, battery, filters, brakes, and tires (including the spare). Consult a qualified vehicle

mechanic if you're not sure what maintenance tasks need to be carried out or when.

78. **Make sure your fuel tank is never less than half-full.** When you see the gauge at half-way, fill it up again. Ask yourself this question: *"If I had to leave town in a hurry, how far could I travel on half a tank of fuel?"* The answer is, *"a lot further than a quarter of a tank or less!"* As a backup, carry one or two empty fuel containers in your vehicle and fill them at the earliest opportunity when you believe a shortage or long lines for fuel is likely. When an out of control wildfire engulfed the Canadian city of Fort McMurray in May 2016, more than 80,000 residents fled for safety and scores of motorists were forced to abandon their vehicles by the roadside when they ran out of fuel. If you abandon your vehicle, be sure to leave a note explaining why and where you are going (see the worksheet at the end of the book).

79. **Identify several evacuation routes on your road maps.** Plan routes to avoid potential hazards such as collapsed bridges, downed power lines, flooded roads, rock slides, areas of heavy vegetation — anything that could impede your escape following a disaster. Practice a mock evacuation with your family by following one of

these routes. Record these routes on the maps or use the worksheet at the end of the book.

80. **Keep a GPS unit in your vehicle** (but not the type that requires Internet access to work) preloaded with the locations of all your evacuation points and meeting places. Since you can't always rely on having a working GPS to assist navigation, keep a set of local, regional and national road maps in your vehicle as well. Mark these maps with the same evacuation routes and meeting places. These printed maps will serve as a reliable backup and you should become familiar with how to read them.

81. **Don't make unnecessary journeys in bad weather.** If you must travel in bad conditions, plan your journey carefully and let others know where you're going and when you expect to return. Never leave home without your personal 72-hour kit and some food and water.

82. **Park your vehicle facing the street.** This has a number of benefits. First, by facing traffic you can exit more quickly and safely than by backing out. Whilst stationed as a refugee relief worker in Thailand, it was standard protocol to park our vehicles facing the exit gates of the camps and leave the keys in the ignition. I'm not

suggesting you leave the keys in your car, but in our situation we had to be ready at a moment's notice to quickly evacuate the camp if it came under attack. Second, if your vehicle refuses to start because of a dead battery or mechanical failure, allowing easier access to the front of the vehicle from the street will help greatly when jump-starting, working on or towing your vehicle.

83. **Carry a set of battery jumper cables** and know how to use them! It always concerns me when I come across people who are stranded with a dead battery and they either don't have jumper cables or know how to use them. Don't stop there... Learn how to change the tires on your car. It's actually surprising how many people don't know how to do this either. Acquiring these simple, yet important skills could become valuable one day.

84. **Keep a simple tool kit in your vehicle**, including screwdrivers, pliers, ratchet set, wire cutters/strippers, hammer, duct tape, electrical tape, zip ties, bungee cords, WD40 lubricant, 9m (30ft) tow strap, hose clamps of various sizes, shop rags, mechanics gloves, headlamp and spare batteries, and your vehicle's repair manual.

85. **Attach a small, colorful flag to your vehicle's antenna.** Have you ever searched the parking lot trying to

remember where you parked your car? Having a highly visual marker can help others find it too if you tell them, *"meet at my car in five minutes, it's the one with the yellow flag on the antenna."* The marker on my truck's radio antenna is made from a strip of high visibility duct tape.

86. **Get a bike for each member of your family.** If all else fails, a bike could become an effective way of getting around. Make sure you know how to perform basic repair tasks such as repairing punctures, fixing brake cables and broken chains.

Discover more disaster transportation ideas at:

www.disaster.zone/resource/transportation

18. Money, Valuables and Documents

"An investment in knowledge pays the best interest."
— Benjamin Franklin

Can you imagine escaping a wildfire and not having any time to pack all the important documents that prove who you are, what you own, or how to reestablish your life? Your "life" documents may be some of the most important items you will need once it's time to get back on your feet again after a disaster.

Don't let a lack of finances prevent you from being better prepared for a disaster. Many steps require little to no financial commitment and there is much you can do to improve your disaster preparedness plan without stretching your budget. But let's be realistic, even before a disaster strikes many people are strapped for cash and struggle to make ends meet. Not everyone in the world has a bank account or easy access to credit. It's vital therefore to build up your *"hands-on assets"* in the form of practical skills such as carpentry, bricklaying, plumbing, general labor, or sewing — all of which can be traded for cash or food in post-disaster recovery efforts.

87. **Make copies of important documents** such as passports, birth certificates, ownership papers and medical records in a safe and secure location, such as a

fireproof and waterproof box or safe, or with a trusted friend or relative. If you keep electronic copies of these documents consider storing them in a password protected format. Create a file of all your important computer sites, usernames and passwords and copy it to a computer USB drive. Protect this important information from identity thieves!

88. **Make a list of all your bank accounts, loans, and credit card details** together with their contact phone numbers. If you have to leave home or your home is destroyed these records may be required to reestablish lines of credit or access funds.

89. **Take photos or record your valuables on video.** Evidence of your possessions will be required when you make insurance claims. Keep the files on a USB drive or CD with your other important documents.

90. **Keep individual photos of your family members in your wallet or purse.** These photos can be used to help emergency services and Search and Rescue (SAR) teams find your loved ones if they are lost.

91. **Create a US$500-$1,000 emergency fund** (or whatever is reasonable in your economy and budget) in a separate *"For Emergencies Only"* bank account. This money will be

used for short- to long-term disaster recovery efforts. Sell the stuff you don't need, take a part-time job and do whatever you can to save up enough for your emergency fund. Start saving today and make it your goal to have this fund ready for when it's needed.

92. **Keep enough spare cash on hand** to pay for food, water, fuel, and other essential supplies. A disaster may disable bank ATM machines so keep some cash available for when normal access to funds is not possible. Make sure your cash reserve is in small denominations. In an emergency, how much do you think a bottle of water will cost if you only have a $10 note and no change is available? You got it – $10!

See the worksheet pages at the end of the book for a list of all the important documents you may need.

Discover more disaster document ideas at:

www.disaster.zone/resource/documents

19. Tools and Repairs

"Get the very best tools to serve your people,

not just lots of tools."

— John Stahl-Wert

Disasters don't play by our rules and since they're usually unexpected, constantly dynamic and chaotic, you will need to be prepared to deal with a variety of different challenges.

One of the best resources you can assemble is a collection of useful tools and supplies for making temporary repairs to your home, to construct makeshift shelters, or whatever else you need to make life more bearable.

93. **A quality folding multi-tool** can be discretely carried on your belt. If you get no other type of tool, this would be the one to get. A folding multi-tool usually incorporates a set of pliers, several types of blade, a pair of scissors, a screwdriver, and a bottle and can opener in one convenient package.

94. **Get some Personal Protective Equipment** (PPE) including steel toe work boots, heavy duty leather work gloves, splash and impact resistant eye goggles, "N95" rated dust masks, and earplugs. You're already dealing with a disaster so don't make things worse by exposing

yourself to further injury requiring medical help that may not be readily available.

95. **Gather a collection of sturdy hand tools.** Many used-goods stores sell tools that are perfectly functional and suitable for your disaster preparedness kit. You'll need at least a heavy duty claw hammer, pry bar, several screwdrivers, an adjustable wrench, *"tongue-and-groove"* pliers, hacksaw and carpenters saw, bolt cutters, small axe, folding shovel, wire cutters, and a utility knife. The use of power tools may not be an option after a disaster, so focus on having a collection of solid, reliable hand tools. Add a headlamp (for making repairs at night), tool belt, tape measure and a few carpenters' pencils.

96. **Gather some sturdy plywood boards** and pre-cut them to the size of your windows. If you need to protect your home from an oncoming storm you can quickly fasten the boards in place. Add a few boxes of nails and screws. Choose different lengths that can be used to batten down doors and windows, join timbers, and construct makeshift shelters.

97. **Duct tape** is the universal tool for securing things. Don't buy the cheap variety — get the type that's really sticky and tough. Zip-ties, bungee cords, needle and thread, a

roll of electrical tape and some "super glue" will help with minor repairs and construction tasks. Keep all these items neatly organized in resealable plastic bags.

98. **Get some nylon parachute cord** or really strong utility rope — at least 30m (100ft). Parachute cord, also known as *"paracord"* or *"550 cord"* has a typical breaking strain of 250kg (550lb) and has multiple uses including building temporary shelters and being able to tease out finer threads for sewing repairs. Obtain a few carabiners to use with you paracord.

99. **Place all your tools and repair supplies in a strong canvas bag** so they can be carried easily and conveniently wherever you need them.

Discover more disaster tools ideas at:

www.disaster.zone/resource/tools

20. Finally... Take Action!

"Thinking will not overcome fear but action will."

— W. Clement Stone

My hope throughout *"Prepared for Disaster"* has been to present many of the basic elements of disaster preparedness without overwhelming you. Armed with this information the choice is now yours.

Are you ready to make a difference?

The final step is to begin putting all this knowledge into action.

100. **Start preparing and sharing today!** It's important that you start putting your disaster preparedness plan into action today. If you implement just two or three of these steps per week, the amount of preparation you can achieve in less than one year will be incredible. Next, become an advocate for disaster preparedness in your community by sharing your plan with family, friends and neighbors.

21. Preparedness Schedule

"I hear and I forget. I see and I remember. I do and I understand."
— Confucius

Great! Now that you've decided to get prepared for disaster and have started to implement some of the steps described in this book. The next thing is to make disaster preparedness a practice.

To help you develop the habit of being prepared I've created a handy checklist you can follow throughout the year.

One-Time

- Assess the most likely threats in your area.
- Assemble your disaster preparedness kits.
- Attend a first aid course.
- Pass your amateur radio exam and buy a two-way radio.
- Buy an emergency generator.
- Buy a water purification unit.

Every Year

- Replace the water in your 55 gallon storage barrel.
- Take a first aid refresher course (every two years).
- Review your disaster plan with your family.
- Get an annual physical with your doctor.
- Read this book again.

Every Six Months

- Review and practice your evacuation routes.
- Check your fire extinguisher levels.
- Check your insurance policies.

Every Four Months

- Check your 72-hour kits. Replace expired food items and swap out clothing for the changing seasons.
- Update your emergency contact numbers.
- Test your emergency generator.
- Check your first aid kits and replace expired items, especially medicines.

Every Month

- Check your flashlight batteries.
- Add more funds to your emergency account.
- Check your vehicle tires and fluid levels.
- Check batteries in smoke and CO detectors.

Every Week

- Add several new food items to your emergency supplies.

Every Day

- Check the fuel level in your vehicles.
- Check the local weather.
- Keep your cell phone charged.

22. Should You Stay or Go?

"Quick decisions are unsafe decisions"

— Sophocles

Leading up to, or following a disaster, the decision to *"shelter-in-place"* or evacuate to a better location is one which should not be taken lightly. Having the foresight, knowledge and ability to make clear decisions particularly when time is not on your side can literally become the difference between life and death.

Sheltering in place is the decision to seek protection from an impending threat by taking refuge at your current or nearby location.

Evacuating is simply the decision to get out of the way of the threat as safely and as quickly as you can.

The immediate threat of a flood, tsunami, wildfire, or toxic chemical spill will almost certainly dictate your need to evacuate to a safer location by any available means. In other circumstances, your life may depend on making the best and most informed choice possible. Aware of the fact that a disaster will probably overwhelm the capacity of the local government to respond adequately to the needs of everyone, it is preferable to shelter-in-place in your primary residence simply because you're likely to have access to far more resources than what you can carry on your back or transport in your vehicle. Furthermore, you're already in familiar surroundings where you can manage the risk with greater confidence. However, in such difficult times there are no guarantees and the final decision will be yours based on the nature of the situation, the most reliable information you have available at the time, and your tolerance for risk.

The decision to shelter-in-place or evacuate should be determined by three general assessments:

1. **Assess the threat.** In many situations the nature and magnitude of the threat itself and not your level of general preparedness will determine the appropriate course of action you should take. For example, if you live in the direct path of an oncoming hurricane, storm surge, flood or wildfire you should evacuate quickly to a safer place. A terrorist attack or other sudden, unforeseen disaster event may present a different set of options. Faced with a life-threatening situation the choice is simple: *"Do I risk losing my life or saving it?"* In some cases, local authorities such as the police, emergency services, or military will make the decision for you by imposing a mandatory shelter-in-place or evacuation order.

2. **Assess your location.** Next, you need to carefully examine your current location and decide if you'll be better off somewhere else or if you should remain where you are. For many people, the shelter-in-place location will be their primary residence such as a house or apartment, located in built-up areas or in the countryside.

Ask yourself the following questions:

- Am I in a location that is likely to withstand the threat?
- Do I have a well-built, defensible home?
- Do I have a storm shelter or other reinforced place to take refuge?
- Do I have access to a source of up-to-date information such as a battery operated radio or T.V.?
- How long might I need to shelter-in-place? Hours, days, weeks, or months?
- Do I have adequate supplies of food and fresh water?
- Do I have access to adequate fuel and alternative energy sources for cooking, heating and lighting?
- Am I relying on a working water or electrical supply over which I have no control?

- Do I have access to tools and supplies to make repairs on my home if necessary?
- Do I have reliable and trustworthy neighbors, and a strong community support network to assist recovery?

3. **Assess your circumstances.** Given the option of sheltering in place or evacuating, you should consider other factors affecting your final decision. Many of these factors will depend on such things as:

- The age, health and mobility of your family members.
- The level of your prior planning.
- Your willingness to leave pets and livestock behind if necessary.

Furthermore, your decision to stay or leave should be based on good information and the ability to answer a number of important questions:

- Is this an emergency or just an inconvenience?
- Can I guarantee the health and safety of myself and my family?
- Do I know where I will go?
- Do I know how I will get there?

- What information do I have about the route I will take?
- Are there people expecting me to arrive?
- Have the authorities imposed travel restrictions?
- Have I made adequate preparations to reach my destination?

You need to be able to answer these assessment questions with a very high degree of confidence. If the answers to any of these questions cannot be easily determined, it may be advisable to stay where you are.

Depending on where you are, your "Shelter-in-Place" plan will help you know what to do to stay safe:

At home. Identify at least one room where you can all shelter safely. Depending on the nature of the threat this room will help protect you from flying debris, dangerous gasses, or flooding. For example, in the case of a toxic gas leak you should choose a room located above ground level. Most chemicals are heavier than air and it would therefore be dangerous to shelter in a basement where gasses would penetrate even if all the windows and doors are sealed. In the event of a tornado you would take shelter in an interior room or below ground level away from flying glass and debris. Ideally, choose a room that has solid walls with few openings. Turn off all utilities, including water, gas and electricity. A gas leak or electrical spark could start a fire. Only turn the utilities back on when you're certain it is safe to do so. Move your vehicle off the street to allow others to navigate the roads more easily.

At work. Close the business. Bring everyone including employees, customers and guests into one or more safe rooms. For example, an interior conference or storage room works well. Shut and lock all the doors, windows and other openings to the outside. If there is any threat from toxic gasses, seal all openings to the safe rooms using duct tape and plastic sheeting. For periods of a few hours, there is little danger of suffocation through lack of oxygen. Unless there is immediate danger, invite everyone present to call their emergency contact and let them know where they are and that they are safe. Write down the names of everyone in the room and their relationship with your business and use this list to call your business' main emergency contact to inform them of your status. All employees and staff should familiarize themselves with company emergency and evacuation procedures.

In your vehicle. If you're in your vehicle when you receive a *shelter-in-place* advisory and are close enough to your home, workplace, or a public building, go there immediately and follow the steps described above. If you're unable to reach your home or workplace quickly and safely, then stop your vehicle in a safe place. If possible, seek a place of shelter from the weather. Call your emergency contacts and let them know where you are. Keep the radio turned on and listen for news updates and instructions. While you wait, formulate at least two possible evacuation routes, being aware that roads may have since become closed and traffic detoured.

You should stay in your vehicle if:

- You're stuck on the road to avoid exposure and/or rescue is likely.
- A safe location is neither nearby nor visible.
- You do not have appropriate clothing to go outside.
- You do not have the ability to call for help.

You should consider finding shelter elsewhere if:

- The shelter is nearby and accessible.
- You have visibility and outside conditions are safe.
- You have appropriate protective clothing.

If evacuation is the only viable option, then do not delay! Gather your family together, pack only the most essential emergency supplies and leave immediately! You should carry out your evacuation plan as quickly as possible to avoid becoming trapped by deteriorating conditions.

Before you evacuate you should make the best efforts to protect your home or workplace. The following checklist will help you plan everything that needs to be done. These tasks can be delegated to different people but make sure everyone knows what their job is and how to do it.

- Account for everyone in the building. Explain what you will be doing and ensure that everyone is aware of the plan. Maintain calm.
- Turn on the news or weather radio to monitor changing conditions.
- Locate your 72-hour kits and gather other evacuation supplies. Put them in your vehicle.
- Prepare your vehicles for evacuation first in case you need to leave at a moment's notice. Make sure the vehicle starts and that you have enough fuel for the journey.
- Find your pets and secure them in one location ready for evacuation.
- Wear sturdy shoes and clothing that will provide protection from the weather.
- Bring outside objects inside. Anything that is not tied down or put away could become a projectile in high winds or carried away in floodwater.
- Close all shutters, blinds and curtains.

- Board up all windows and openings to protect against flying debris.
- Disconnect all electrical appliances and other equipment that cannot be moved.
- If flooding is likely, move furniture and other moveable objects to upper floors.
- Shut off all utilities to the house including water, electricity and gas.
- Lock away all valuables.
- Close all windows and lock all doors.
- Park unused vehicles in the garage or driveway.
- Leave a note to alert others when you left and where you're planning to go. Provide a contact phone number if possible.

In the final analysis, the decision to shelter-in-place or seek a safer location will require placing the health and safety of your family before anything else. People are more important than things. You can always replace your stuff, but you should never take chances with the lives and well-being of your loved ones.

23. What to Do in a Disaster?

"Chance favors only the prepared mind."

Louis Pasteur

Being prepared by having a supply of essential and useful disaster preparedness items is all well and good. But what do you *actually do* to prepare for and survive specific natural disaster situations? Perhaps you purchased this book out of general curiosity but now you're reading the pages in this section because you're about to face a very real and immediate threat. This section is intended to be a quick and handy reference for common types of disaster.

Power Outages

The loss of power following a disaster is quite common. This may be due to the electrical infrastructure being damaged, or disconnected because of safety concerns. For example, electrical power will be cut-off if there is any danger of causing ruptured gas lines to explode or harming rescue workers.

Before a power outage

What types of electrical appliance do you need power for and what types can you live without? Having backup electrical power for lighting and communications may be more important than needing electricity for cooking. Whenever possible, avoid using an open flame for light or heat. The last thing you want on your hands is a secondary disaster caused by careless handling of flammable liquids or gas!

- Take a careful inventory of what you need and ensure you have alternative power sources available, such as disposable batteries or a solar power system.
- Stockpile enough batteries for your flashlights, radios, etc. and make sure they are the correct size.
- If you need a screwdriver to open a battery-operated device make sure you know where it is located. Make sure these items have fresh batteries installed and are ready for use.
- Keep a supply of flashlights, batteries, candles, matches and glow-sticks in strategic locations such as kitchen drawers and entrance ways.
- Ideally, each person in your household should have their own flashlight.
- If you have a gas barbeque grill, make sure you always have at least one full, spare gas cylinder on hand.
- If you plan to use an electrical generator, make sure you know how it works before you actually need it. Ensure you have enough fuel stored safely. Don't forget the operator's manual, engine oil, spare spark plugs, extension cords and any adapters you may need. Be aware of the electrical limits of the generator. For

example, don't expect a small 1,000 watt generator to power a large family fridge-freezer.

- Does your hardwired home or office phone work without power? Consider getting a simple phone handset (not a cordless model) that can plug directly into the wall adapter and use the phone system's own power to make calls.
- Ensure your cell phones are always charged.
- Know where the electrical shut-off switch to your home or workplace is located.
- Practice an evening without power. Inform your family that there will be a power cut. Cut the power and discover how people react. Use this as a valuable learning experience.
- If someone in your household is dependent on electrical power for life-sustaining medical equipment, make sure you have a backup generator and an evacuation plan.

During a power outage

- Remain calm. Try to determine what caused the power outage. Your battery powered or hand-crank radio may provide the information you need.
- Locate working and spare batteries.

- Only use candles and other open flame devices as a last resort when safe to do so. Never use open flames if you can smell gas or other fuels.

- Disconnect important electrical appliances so they are protected from power surges once the electrical supply is reestablished but keep one light switched "on" so you know when power has been restored.

- Disable nonessential features on your cell phone such as Wi-Fi and Bluetooth. There's no point wasting vital phone battery power on things you can't connect to.

- Locate your emergency generator and fuel. Hook everything up and prepare it for use. Remember to only operate a generator outdoors in a well-ventilated area.

- Remove any obstacles and items from passageways that would otherwise cause a hazard when navigating in the dark.

- Give glow sticks to young children. Not only will they have their own safe source of light, but the novelty and fun will help reassure them.

- If you rely on electricity to pump water, start conserving water immediately.

- Place some tape on refrigerator and freezer doors to hold them shut. This will help remind people not to open them and thereby prolong the life of your perishable food items. An unopened refrigerator will keep food cold for about four hours. A full freezer will keep the temperature at a safe level for about 48 hours, or about a day if it's half full.

- If the power outage is likely to last for more than a few days, plan to consume as much of the food in your refrigerator before it spoils. Heavier and denser items in your freezer such as joints of meat are likely to keep longer.
- Move as many items to the bottom of your upright fridge/freezer where it is cooler.
- Keep all other food items in a cool, dry area and covered at all times.
- In cold environments, confine your living quarters to a few rooms. Close all windows and doors to conserve heat. Gather extra blankets and clothing to stay warm.
- In hot environments, move to the coolest part of the house, typically a basement or well-shaded area. Avoid strenuous activity especially during the heat of the day. Drink plenty of fluids.
- In a prolonged power outage you may want to adjust your sleep patterns to take advantage of more daylight hours and to sleep with younger children who may otherwise be afraid to sleep in the dark.

- Eliminate any unnecessary travel by car since streetlights will be out and non-functional traffic lights are likely to cause traffic congestion.
- Check on your neighbors, especially the elderly and disabled.

After a power outage

- Report any downed power lines to local authorities.
- Don't touch any power lines or go near them.
- Discard any food that has been exposed to temperatures greater than 4°C (40°F) for more than two hours, has a bad smell, color, or texture, or feels warm to the touch. Never determine if food is safe to eat by its taste, appearance or smell. If in doubt, throw it out!
- Replenish your supplies of batteries, candles, matches, glow sticks, cooking gas and generator fuel as soon as you can.

Severe Storms

Typhoons, cyclones, hurricanes and tornados are types of storm system that deliver their harm in up to three ways: by water, waves, or wind.

What to do before a storm

- Buy flood insurance.

- Consider building a reinforced safe room.
- Reinforce structures with straps and tie-downs, especially the roof.
- Tie down or securely store any loose items that could be blown around, for example outside furniture, garden items and garbage cans.
- Pull your boat out of the water and tie it down.
- Board up windows with 1.5 cm (⅝ in) thick plywood boards. Cut these boards in advance to match the exact size of your windows. Tape will not prevent window glass from breaking. Boarding up windows will also act as a deterrent to looting if you have to evacuate.
- Prepare sandbags to help prevent water entering your basement.
- Clear blocked gutters, downspouts and drainage channels.
- Monitor your local radio station for up-to-date news and weather reports.
- Determine a safe evacuation route.
- Prepare your vehicle for evacuation. If you plan to escape the path of the storm, leave as early as you can to avoid being trapped by weather.
- Gather your disaster supplies kit.
- If instructed to do so, turn off utilities.
- Turn off propane tanks.

- Prepare your electrical generator for use later. Never use a generator indoors!
- Seek safe shelter. Go to an interior safe room away from windows but stay away from low lying areas that are prone to flooding.
- Check on your neighbors, especially the elderly and disabled.

What to do during a storm

- Listen to your radio for news updates and weather reports.
- Close and lock all windows and doors including interior doors.
- Close all curtains and blinds.
- Stay indoors and keep away from windows and doors.
- Unplug electrical appliances, particularly in areas vulnerable to flooding or prone to lightning.
- Seek shelter in an interior room, closet or hallway. Lie on the floor, under a table or other sturdy object.
- Avoid using the phone except in an emergency.
- Do not use an elevator.
- If you're in a vehicle during a tornado and forced to pull over, stay in the vehicle with your seatbelt on. Lower your head below the windows and cover your head with your hands or a jacket.

What to do after a storm

- Continue to monitor your local news for important updates.
- Do not enter an affected area until it's declared safe.
- Avoid flooded roads and obstacles. Be cautious of weakened bridges and overhangs.
- Stay away from downed power lines.
- If necessary, turn off utilities such as water, electricity and gas.
- Do not enter a building if you smell gas or fuel.
- Wear sturdy footwear and protective clothing when inspecting damage.
- Use a flashlight to inspect damage. Open flames increase the risk of explosion or fire if there are gas leaks or spilled fuel.
- Be aware of wild animals and poisonous snakes amongst debris.
- Check on your neighbors, especially the elderly and disabled.

Winter Storms

A winter storm is an event in which different types of precipitation form at low temperatures, such as snow or sleet, or where ground temperatures are low enough to form freezing rain.

What to do before a snowstorm

- Before winter approaches, add the following items to your emergency supplies:
    - Rock salt (halite / sodium chloride crystals) or similar products to melt ice on paths and walkways.
    - Sand to improve traction.
    - Snow shovels and other snow removal equipment.
    - A good supply of heating fuel for your fireplace or stove.
    - Adequate clothing and warm blankets.
- Minimize travel, but whenever you venture out in your vehicle take along a disaster supplies kit.
- Bring pets inside. Move other animals and livestock to sheltered areas with non-frozen drinking water.
- Insulate your home and protect water pipes from freezing.

What to do during a snowstorm

- Stay indoors and stay warm.
- Walk carefully on snow and ice-covered walkways.

- Avoid overexertion when shoveling snow. Overexertion can bring on a heart attack. Exercise caution, take breaks, and push the snow instead of lifting it.
- Keep dry. Wet clothing will quickly sap body heat. Change wet clothing frequently to prevent the risk of hypothermia.
- Drive only if it is absolutely necessary. If you must drive, do so during the day on well used roads and avoid shortcuts. Let someone know your destination, your route, and when you expect to arrive. If your car gets stranded, help can be sent along your predetermined route.
- Maintain proper ventilation when using kerosene heaters to avoid build-up of toxic fumes. Refuel kerosene heaters outside and at least 1m (3ft) from flammable objects.
- Temporarily shut off heat to some rooms to conserve fuel. If you plan to be away during cold weather, leave the heat on in your home and set it to a temperature no less than 13°C (55°F).

If a blizzard traps you in the car:

- Pull off the highway. Turn on hazard lights and hang a distress flag from the radio antenna or window. If possible, call someone on your phone to let them know where you are.

- Remain in your vehicle where rescuers are most likely to find you. Do not set out on foot unless you can see a building close by where you know you can take shelter. Be careful though – distances are often distorted by blowing snow. A building may appear close by, but be too far to walk in deep snow.

- Run the engine and heater for about ten minutes each hour to keep warm and keep the car battery charged. When the engine is running, open a downwind window slightly for ventilation and periodically clear snow from the exhaust pipe to protect you from carbon monoxide poisoning.

- Exercise to maintain body heat, but avoid overexertion. In extreme cold, use whatever you have at hand (maps, seat covers, floor mats, etc.) for insulation. Huddle with fellow passengers and use your coat as a blanket.

- Take turns sleeping. One person should stay awake to look for rescuers.

- Eat regularly and drink sufficient fluids (preferably water) to avoid dehydration. Avoid caffeine and alcohol.

- Be careful not to rundown the car's battery or fuel. Keep your cell phone charged.

- Turn on the inside light at night so workers or rescuers can see you.
- If stranded in a remote area, stomp large letters in an open area spelling out **HELP** or **SOS** and line with rocks or tree limbs to attract the attention of rescuers who may be searching the area by plane.

Floods

Flooding occurs when water, usually from a river or stream overflows and inundates the surrounding land that is normally dry. Flooding can also occur in coastal areas when a large storm or tsunami causes the sea to surge inland. The force of flowing water has incredible destructive power causing buildings and bridges to become unstable by undermining their foundations.

What to do before a flood

- Find out as much as you can about your home's susceptibility to flooding. Consult a local "floodplain map".
- If necessary, buy flood insurance since your homeowner's insurance may not cover flood damage.
- Move the heating furnace, water heater, and electric panels above the high water mark.
- Install sewage line "check valves" to prevent floodwater from backing up into your home.

- Construct flood barriers to prevent floodwater from entering your home.
- Apply waterproofing compounds to basement walls to avoid water seepage.
- Install an attic or rooftop ladder.
- Stockpile extra bottled drinking water.

What to do during a flood

- Listen for information updates on your battery-powered radio or T.V.
- Move immediately to higher ground if there is any danger of a flash flood. If water rises in your home before you're able to evacuate, go to the top floor, attic, or roof.
- Be aware that streams, drainage channels, canyons, and other areas are sometimes prone to flash floods with or without warning signs such as rain clouds or heavy downpours.
- Turn off utilities at the main switches or valves. To avoid the risk of electrocution, disconnect all electrical appliances, especially those in low-lying areas. Do not touch any electrical equipment if you're wet or standing in water.
- Secure your home contents by moving essential items to an upper floor. If you have time, bring in outdoor furniture.

- Do not attempt to walk through flowing water. Even a 15 cm (6 in) depth of moving water is enough to cause someone to lose their balance. If you have to walk through water, go to where the water is not moving and use a sturdy stick to check the ground in front of you.
- Do not drive into flooded areas. If you become surrounded by floodwaters, abandon your vehicle and move to higher ground only if it's safe to do so.

What to do after a flood

- Listen to the radio for information and return home only when it is safe.
- Be aware of areas where floodwaters have receded. Roads may have weakened and could collapse under the weight your vehicle.
- Stay out of any buildings surrounded by floodwaters. When you're able to enter a building use extreme caution since there may be hidden damage, particularly in foundations.
- Avoid floodwater which may be contaminated by chemicals and raw sewage or electrically charged from underground or downed power lines.
- Stay away from broken power lines and report damage to the power company.

- Do not turn power back on until it has been safety-inspected by an electrician.
- Find out if your local water supply is safe to drink. If in doubt, don't drink it.
- Clean and disinfect everything that got wet. Floodwater often contains sewage and harmful chemicals.
- Take photos of any flood damage and call your insurance company as soon as possible to file a claim.
- Check on your neighbors, especially the elderly and disabled.

Wildfires

A wildfire is an uncontrollable countryside fire in an area of highly combustible vegetation. Wildfires usually cover a wide area, spread very quickly, are liable to change direction unexpectedly, and can jump gaps such as roads, fire breaks, and even rivers.

What to do before a wildfire

- Create a defensible space to separate your home from flammable vegetation and materials.
- Trim trees and shrubs to prevent them coming into contact with electrical wires or overhang your chimney. Do not attempt to trim around power lines yourself – call the power company.

- Keep roof surfaces and gutters clear of pine needles, leaves and debris at all times.
- Prune all lower branches 2.5m (8ft) from the ground and keep the trees adjacent to buildings free of dead or dying branches. Mow grass regularly.
- Cut back tree branches and shrubs within 4.5m (15ft) of a stovepipe or chimney outlet and remove vines from the walls.
- Clean chimneys and check and maintain spark arresters twice a year.
- Use approved fire resistant materials when building, repairing or retrofitting structures.
- Be sure your house number is clearly visible from the street, both day and night. This will help emergency services find you more easily.
- Remove leaves and rubbish from under structures, and store combustible or flammable (such as a woodpile) safely uphill away from main buildings.
- Clear a 3m (10ft) area around propane tanks and the barbecue grill.

What to do during a wildfire

- Monitor your radio for the latest emergency information.
- Be prepared to evacuate your family and pets when instructed to do so or if you feel in danger.

- Disconnect any automatic garage door openers so that doors can still be opened by hand if the power goes out. Reverse your car and leave the keys in the ignition. Close all garage doors.

- Place valuable documents and important belongings (family photos, jewelry, etc.) inside the car in the garage, ready for a quick departure. Any pets still with you should also be secured in the car. Place valuables that will not be damaged by water in a swimming pool or pond.

- Wear protective clothing when outside – sturdy shoes, cotton or woolen clothes, long pants, a long-sleeved shirt, gloves, and a handkerchief to protect your face.

- Limit your time outdoors and practice safe driving. Be aware of smoke on roads because it could decrease visibility.

- If you have a ladder, prop it against the house so you and firefighters have access to the roof.

- If hoses and adequate water are available, set them up. Fill buckets and other large containers with water.

- If you have gas-powered pumps for water, make sure they are fueled and ready for use.

- Gather firefighting tools such as a rake, axe, handsaw or chainsaw, bucket and shovel.

- Remove combustible materials from the area surrounding your house such as lawn chairs, benches, and tables.
- Shut off any natural gas, propane or fuel oil supplies at the source.
- Place lawn sprinklers on the roof and near above-ground fuel tanks. Leave sprinklers on to douse structures as long as possible.
- Close all doors and windows, but do not lock them. Close all interior doors to prevent draft. Open the damper on your fireplace, but close the fireplace screen.
- Open or take down flammable drapes and curtains, and close all venetian blinds and non-flammable window coverings to reduce radiant heat.
- Move flammable furniture into the center of the residence away from the windows and sliding-glass doors.
- Turn off air conditioning/air circulation systems.
- Turn on outside lights and leave a light on in every room to make the house more visible in heavy smoke.

What to do after a wildfire

- If you're with burn victims, or are a burn victim yourself, seek medical help immediately. Cool and cover burns to reduce the chance of further injury or infection.

- If you remained at home, check the roof immediately after the fire danger has passed.
- Avoid damaged or fallen power lines, poles and downed wires.
- Wear protective equipment to prevent harm to your hands, feet, and limbs. Wear a face mask.
- Use caution when entering a burned area since flare-ups can occur. If you detect heat or smoke when entering a damaged building, evacuate immediately.
- Check the grounds for hot-spots, smoldering tree stumps and vegetation. Douse these areas with buckets of water. Continue to check for problem areas for several days.
- Watch animals closely and keep them under your direct control. Hidden embers and hot spots could burn your pet's paws or hooves.
- Check the roof, attic, house and exterior areas for sparks and embers.
- Go to a designated public shelter if you have been told to evacuate or you feel it is unsafe to remain in your home.
- Do not open your safe or strong box. They can retain intense heat for several hours. If the door is opened before the box has cooled, the contents could burst into flames.
- Wet-down debris to minimize airborne dust particles.

- Throw away any food that has been exposed to heat, smoke or soot.

- Do not use any water that you think may be contaminated to clean dishes, prepare food or drinks, wash hands or your brush teeth.

Earthquakes

The tectonic plates that make up the Earth's surface are in constant motion. Millions of *"micro"* earthquakes happen each year around the world but they are so small and have little concern or consequence. Unlike most other types of disaster, large earthquakes, the ones which cause significant damage in urban areas, cannot easily be predicted. Scientific methods can teach us that a deadly earthquake is likely to happen at some point in time, but we will never know the *exact* moment it will strike. Therefore, the precautions you can take are related to minimizing the level of damage they will cause to property and human life.

Earthquakes in heavily populated areas are likely to cause many deaths and injuries, and considerable property damage. Roads, bridges, railways and other important infrastructure, and essential services such as hospitals may be badly damaged. The further effect of fires, flash-flooding, landslides, avalanches and tsunamis can have a much wider impact far away from the actual epicenter of the earthquake. Furthermore, the effect of smaller earthquakes or *"aftershocks"* can continue for many days, weeks, or months after the initial event or herald the arrival of an even greater earthquake!

Most types of damage caused by earthquakes are predictable and can be prevented by taking measures to minimize catastrophic property damage.

When I was in Haiti in January 2010, shortly after the massive 7.0 magnitude earthquake, I was surprised to see some streets where buildings had collapsed and been reduced to piles of rubble. And yet, on the very same street other buildings had sustained only light damage. I soon learned that it was how the buildings had been designed and built that determined which ones remained standing and which ones ultimately crumbled. In many cases building regulations were not observed and corners had been cut to save construction costs, resulting in huge losses of life. The earthquake claimed an estimated 100,000 to 160,000 lives. By contrast, an 8.8 magnitude earthquake that struck Chile the following month killed 525 people! Many attribute the massive difference in losses to Chile's observance of strict building codes and Haiti's widespread lack of safe building practices. The saying, *"It's not earthquakes that kill people, but the buildings that fall on them!"* is very true.

What to do before an earthquake

- Have a qualified engineer inspect your building. If necessary, relocate your family to a safer building, otherwise reinforce the structure and ensure your home is securely anchored to its foundations.
- Secure all loose items to the wall. A good rule of thumb is that anything that is taller than it is wide and not secured to the wall is likely to fall over.
- Repair any defective electrical wiring.
- Place large, heavy objects on lower shelves.
- Fasten shelves, mirrors and large picture frames to walls.
- Remove items hanging over your bed or likely to block an escape route.
- Store bottled foods and other breakable items on lower shelves or within cabinets that can be fastened shut.
- Install child safety latches on cupboard doors to help prevent items from spilling out during a quake.
- Secure overhead lighting fixtures.
- Know where and how to shut off utility connections such as gas, water and electricity.
- Install an automatic gas shut-off valve that closes when seismic vibrations are detected.
- Locate safe zones within your home where you can shelter such as beneath a study table or against an inside wall.

- Keep a flashlight, a bottle of drinking water, a small backpack of disaster preparedness items, and a good pair of shoes by your bed. When you need to escape, the last thing you want is to be stepping on broken glass in your bare feet in the dark.

- Practice earthquake drills with your family and co-workers. Test your families' skill and ability to quickly find safe locations within your home.

- Relying on unusual animal or bird behavior to indicate an impending earthquake is anecdotal at best and not particularly scientific.

- Practice the *"Drop! Cover! Hold!"* earthquake drill:
   - ○ **Drop!** Drop down to the floor.
   - ○ **Cover!** Protect yourself by finding overhead protection such as a desk, table, work bench, or the corner of a room away from windows.
   - ○ **Hold!** Hold on to something sturdy like a piece of solid furniture or get next to an interior wall. Be prepared to move with it until the shaking stops.

What to do during an earthquake

- **If you're inside a building:**
   - ○ Drop down, find cover and hold on.

- Stay inside until the shaking stops. Move as little as possible and stay still until you believe it's safe to go outside.
- Stay away from glass, windows, outside doors or walls and anything that could fall.
- If you're in bed, stay there and protect your head with a pillow.
- If there isn't a table or desk nearby, crouch down in an inside corner of the building and cover your face and head with your arms.
- A doorway should only be used for shelter if you're certain it's a load bearing structure and if not everyone in the room is rushing for the same doorway!

- **If you're in an apartment or office building:**
  - Follow the same steps as above.
  - Do not use the elevator! Take the stairs.

- **If you're in a crowded indoor public location:**
  - Stay where you are.
  - Do not rush for a doorway where you may be trampled by other people.
  - Move away from any tall objects that may fall.
  - Take cover. Squat down and shield your head from falling glass and debris.

- A safe place to find shelter is beneath a heavy desk or between sturdy pieces of furniture. If there is no obvious safe place, move to an inside corner away from windows or mirrors.
- Take the stairs. Never use an elevator!

- **If you're outside:**
  - Stay outside. Move away from buildings, overhangs, streetlights and power lines.

- **If you're in a moving vehicle:**
  - Stop as quickly and as safely as you can. Pull over to the side of the road.
  - Avoid stopping near or beneath buildings, trees, bridges, or utility wires.
  - Stay in your vehicle and keep your seatbelt on.
  - If you're in a mountainous area, near a slope or a cliff, be on alert for falling rock or debris. Earthquakes often start landslides.
  - Proceed carefully, watching for road and bridge damage.

- **If you become trapped in debris:**
  - Do not light a match or use a lighter! Use the mini-flashlight on your keyring.
  - Do not move around or kick up dust.

o Cover your mouth with a handkerchief or clothing.

o Tap on a pipe or wall so rescuers can locate you.

o Save your breath and use a whistle if you have one. Three short bursts of sound will alert others of your location.

o Shout only as a last resort — shouting can cause you to inhale too much dust.

What to do after an earthquake

- Be prepared for aftershocks, landslides and fires which may cause additional damage.

- Get out of the building and seek a safe location away from falling debris.

- If you live near the coast, move to higher ground immediately. The earthquake may cause a tsunami wave.

- Watch the ground for broken glass and other debris. Put on sturdy shoes.

- Check for injuries and perform necessary first aid.

- If the electricity goes out, use a flashlight. Do not use any naked flames.

- Clean up spilled chemicals, medicines, fuel or other flammable liquids.

- Evacuate the building if you smell gas and the building is not well ventilated.

- Shut off all utilities, especially gas and electricity.
- Extinguish any small fires.
- Do not flush toilets unless you're certain the sewer lines are undamaged.
- Open cupboards carefully. Objects may fall down.
- Only use the phone to report life threatening emergencies.
- Stay off the streets. When you must go outside, watch for fallen objects, power lines, weakened walls and other structures.
- Stay away from damaged areas.
- Be aware of animals that may become aggressive after an earthquake.
- Check on your neighbors, especially the elderly and disabled.

Tsunamis

"Tsunami" is the Japanese word meaning *"harbor wave."* They are usually caused when an earthquake occurs beneath a large body of water. The surface of the water is displaced and eventually causes large waves to hit land many hundreds or thousands of miles away from the quake's epicenter. As the rapidly moving waves approach the shallow coastal waters, they appear normal but their speed decreases significantly. The

compression of the wave resulting from the decrease in ocean depth causes the wave to grow higher and crash onto land.

Tsunamis can also be caused by landslides, volcanic eruptions and explosions. Locally generated tsunamis leave very little time for people to act upon warning systems.

What to do before a tsunami

- If you feel an earthquake in a coastal area, leave the beach or low-lying areas immediately. Turn on your radio and listen for a tsunami warning.
- The following terms are used to describe tsunami warnings:
    - **Advisory** — an earthquake has occurred which might generate a tsunami.
    - **Watch** — a tsunami was or may have been generated and may arrive within at least two hours.
    - **Warning** — a tsunami was or may have been generated which could cause damage. People are advised to evacuate the area.
- Listen to your radio or T.V. for announcements.
- If available, subscribe to a tsunami warning text alert service on your mobile phone.

- An immediate sign of a tsunami is a noticeable recession in water from the shoreline. Move inland and to higher ground immediately.
- Understand that the topography of the coastline and the ocean floor can mean that a small tsunami at one beach can mean a much larger one elsewhere.
- A tsunami may generate more than one wave. If the first wave seems relatively harmless, be warned that the next may be bigger and more deadly.
- Get ready to put your evacuation plan into action.

What to do during a tsunami

- If you're advised to evacuate, do so immediately!
- Stay away from the beach and low lying areas. Seek higher ground immediately.

What to do after a tsunami

- Stay away from flooded areas until they're declared safe.
- Stay away from debris in the water.

Epilogue

"By failing to prepare, you are preparing to fail."
— **Benjamin Franklin**

No one is immune to disaster. In today's troubled world the threat is very real, can happen at any time, and come at you from any direction. Being prepared to deal with a disaster is not just the responsibility for *"the experts"* or *"the fanatical"*. Disasters don't affect just those types of people — they can affect anyone... including you!

When you're prepared for the worst you're in a position of strength, not only to help yourself and your family, but to be of greater service to your immediate neighbors and the wider community. The truth is, I hope you will never need to use the advice presented in this book, but at such a time you will be glad you took the steps to be prepared. Your family, friends, co-workers and neighbors will be grateful as they look to you for inspiration, leadership and direction.

If you have enjoyed this book and found it useful, please tell your friends about it and leave a positive review where you purchased it. This will really help spread the word and help others get prepared for a disaster.

Finally, please visit my website at www.disaster.zone to discover more disaster preparedness tips and ideas.

Thanks, and stay safe!

Steve Neill

Discover more disaster preparedness resources online:

WWW.DISASTER.ZONE

About The Author

Steve Neill is a UK native who has traveled the globe extensively. He spends much of his spare time writing disaster related materials and building portable water purification systems for disaster responders. Humanitarian issues and clean water are subjects he is very passionate about.

In 1987 at the age of 19, Steve traveled to Thailand to volunteer with an organization called Youth With A Mission. *"I was young and inexperienced, but eager to learn all I could about the plight of refugees living in Thailand,"* says Steve. *"I volunteered as a handyman to fix broken doors and lights. I worked with a large team of doctors and health workers in a small Thai border town. We often heard the fighting between the Khmer Rouge and Vietnamese forces across the border and had to familiarize ourselves with security protocols to avoid putting ourselves in danger. It was quite an eye-opener!"*

Steve recounts the time he visited the refugee camp called Site Two. *"One of my first impressions was the crowds of people with nowhere to go. The camp was hot and exposed. I remember seeing crowds of men, women, and children gathering around water collection points. The constant sight of leaky United Nations trucks making daily trips to provide chlorinated water to the thousands of refugees helped me realize that water was obviously a big deal."*

"During my first time in Thailand, I visited the Burmese border to meet Karen refugees. These refugees were scattered across numerous camps, many inaccessible by road during the rainy season. For many of these wonderful people, their living conditions were basic. I was able to stay on the camps and live in their bamboo shelters. I drank a lot of boiled water and thankfully never got sick. The biggest threat it seemed was from malaria though I did see many people with intestinal issues."

Steve made almost thirty visits to Thailand working as a freelance photojournalist and to deliver relief aid to Karen refugees from Myanmar.

"On my many travels and despite being as careful as possible, I could never guarantee the quality of the water or food I was consuming. The worst time however, was when I got really sick with dengue fever. I was working on the Thai/Cambodian border

when I experienced the worst headaches and energy-sapping fatigue I've ever had. It was awful," recalls Steve. *"After that experience I became an advocate for adding small guppy fish to all the water containers we used for washing and flushing our toilets — the fish ate the malaria and dengue mosquito larvae and thus mitigated further sickness within the team."*

Steve quickly gained an understanding of the various dimensions of disaster relief during his many visits to refugee camps, disaster zones and by attending various conferences and seminars. *"One of the things you learn very quickly is that without access to clean water and sanitation you can forget about being successful in other areas of relief aid. If kids are sick because of diarrhea, their education suffers. If a parent can't work because of illness, the whole family suffers. Water is the backbone to supporting other relief and recovery efforts."*

Responding to Cyclone Nargis in Myanmar in 2008, Steve started a non-profit organization called Community Aid Relief and Development (CoAid). *"We just wanted to start helping people in whatever way we could. The first project we did was to give each child in a refugee school their own pair of shoes and an umbrella. Many of these kids only had one set of clothes so the umbrella kept them dry on their walk to school during the rainy season. The shoes helped protect their feet from getting hookworm. It was a low-cost, high-impact project."*

Within a year of starting the non-profit, Community Aid was voted one of the top 100 USA charities in an online poll and won $25,000 from Chase Bank. *"That was a significant boost to our morale and work. We were able to do a lot of good with that money."*

In January 2010, Community Aid responded to the massive earthquake that struck Haiti. Once again Steve found himself in the middle of a disaster zone. *"People were desperate for good water. It was a common theme at the UN cluster meetings,"* recalls Steve.

Just after the Haiti cholera outbreak in October 2010, Community Aid partnered with other disaster relief organizations to set up clean drinking water tanks in a few IDP (internally displaced person) camps. *"We supplied several hundred families with safe, clean water each day and probably saved a few lives in the process."*

Steve's experience with Community Aid and with other disaster response organizations in USA, New Zealand, Thailand, Myanmar, India, Nepal, Africa, Haiti, Costa Rica, Romania and Switzerland has given him strong insights into the practical needs of disaster victims.

In 2013, Steve founded AidGear (www.aidgear.com), a for-profit company to develop portable water purification units for disaster responders. *"Our goal is to build the type of reliable equipment I would want to take with me to the field. Staying healthy in a disaster zone is too important to leave to chance. Saving lives is AidGear's first priority."*

Steve currently lives along the Front Range of the Rocky Mountains in Colorado, USA with his wife Cheri, their two young children, and four cats.

For training and consultancy services please email Steve at: **info@disaster.zone**

Disaster Preparedness Worksheets

Please use the worksheets on the following pages for your disaster preparedness planning. Make as many photocopies of each form as needed. Fill out the required information, and add them to your disaster kits.

Discover more disaster preparedness worksheets at:

www.disaster.zone/resource/worksheets

Important Phone Numbers

Name	Number
Emergency Services	
Police	
Fire	
Ambulance	
Utilities	
Electricity	
Gas	
Water	
Medical	
Doctor	
Dentist	
Hospital	
Immediate Family	
Work	
Work	
School	
School	
Childcare	
Extended Family & Friends	
Neighbor	
Neighbor	
Baby Sitter	
Local contact	
Local contact	
Out of town contact	
Out of town contact	
Other	

Medications

Family Member	Medication	Dosage

Allergies

Family Member	Allergy	Reaction

Important Documents

Document	✔
Adoption papers	
Annual tax statements	
Bank details (account and phone numbers)	
Bank statements	
Beneficiary instructions	
Birth and death certificates	
Computer account logins and passwords	
Credit card copy (front and back)	
Disability records	
Driver's licenses	
Educational records and certificates	
Home improvement documents and receipts	
Home inventory records (list, photos, video)	
House titles	
Immigration and citizenship documents	
Insurance documents	
Investment records	
Marriage license / divorce papers	
Medical and burial instructions	
Medical bills and claims	
Medical insurance documents	
Medical records	
Military discharge papers	
Mortgage documents	
Passports	
Power of attorney letters	
Receipts for major purchases	
Recent family photographs (of individuals)	
Recent paycheck stubs	
Retirement plan records	
Social security cards	
Vehicle descriptions (make, model, VIN, license number)	
Vehicle titles	
Veterinary records for pets	
Welfare documents	
Wills	

★ ★ ATTENTION ★ ★

Due to an emergency I have evacuated this building:

Date and Time: _____

Address: _____

Name: _____

Phone Number: _____

Travel Plans: _____

_____

_____

_____

_____

_____

_____

**Please confirm I have reached the following
destination before discarding this message:**

Contact Name: _____

Contact Phone Number: _____

Contact Address: _____

_____

Due to an emergency I have abandoned this vehicle:

Reason: (No fuel) (Mechanical problem) (Other)

_____

Date and Time: _____   License #: _____

Name: _____

Phone Number: _____

Passenger Info: _____

Travel Plans: _____

_____

_____

_____

_____

_____

Please confirm I have reached the following
destination before discarding this message:

Contact Name: _____

Contact Phone Number: _____

Contact Address: _____

www.disaster.zone/resource/worksheets

Family Meeting Places

1) If we become separated, we will meet at:

_____

_____

_____

_____

_____

2) If the 1st place is not safe, we will meet at:

_____

_____

_____

_____

3) If the 2nd place is not safe, we will meet at:

_____

_____

_____

_____

Evacuation Route

If we need to evacuate by vehicle, take this route:

_____

_____

_____

_____

_____

_____

_____

Map: